The Kids Are Smart Enough, so What's the Problem?

The Kids Are Smart Enough, so What's the Problem?

A Businessman's Perspective on Educational Reform and the Teacher Crisis

Richard W. Garrett

ROWMAN & LITTLEFIELD
Lanham • Boulder • New York • London

Published by Rowman & Littlefield
A wholly owned subsidiary of The Rowman & Littlefield Publishing Group, Inc.
4501 Forbes Boulevard, Suite 200, Lanham, Maryland 20706
www.rowman.com

Unit A, Whitacre Mews, 26–34 Stannary Street, London SE11 4AB

British Library Cataloguing in Publication Information Available

Library of Congress Cataloging-in-Publication Data Available

ISBN: 978-1-4758-3875-6 (cloth : alk. paper)
ISBN: 978-1-4758-3876-3 (pbk. : alk. paper)
ISBN: 978-1-4758-3877-0 (electronic)

♾™ The paper used in this publication meets the minimum requirements of American National Standard for Information Sciences—Permanence of Paper for Printed Library Materials, ANSI/NISO Z39.48–1992.

Printed in the United States of America.

This book is dedicated to:
All teachers who truly want to teach
All students who truly want to learn

Contents

Preface

In public school classrooms throughout America, a percentage of students are seriously disrupting the education of their fellow students. For most of you, this will not come as a surprise, but you will probably be guessing at the impact they have on the teachers and the educational system. You will not hear about this problem from educators because it is politically dangerous for them. The silence from the world of education may leave the false impression that everything is under control, but this is far from the truth.

Data is presented to support the fact that this is a national problem, and you will read about an example case study, using real teachers and real students, to quantify the magnitude of the problem for four fourth-grade classes, at one elementary school, here in Marion County, Indiana (Indianapolis).

You will be surprised at the amount of lost instructional time; you may be also surprised to find that many of the disruptive students are unmanageable by most teachers. Most importantly, we present positive examples of how to reach these struggling students. Generally, this book is full of hope; if we know the real problem, we can probably fix it, but we will need to rise out of our apathy to get this done.

WHY LISTEN TO A BUSINESSMAN?

This book presents the perspective of an outside businessman considering the complicated and vast world of America's pre-K to 12 educational system. It is a bit dangerous and yet possibly very advantageous to listen to someone like me. The danger comes from a lack of depth; the advantages come from hearing a different perspective from someone who is not tainted by political or organizational proclivities.

What's more, I am the father of an elementary teacher, have many close friends who are or were teachers, and I enjoy teaching as well. Combine this with a research-based PhD and a long work history that deals with solving corporate problems, consulting, and work as a university professor; I come to this point well prepared.

A DEBT TO PAY

Northwestern University granted me a PhD in operations research in 1968. Northwestern is a first-class institution that, by any measure, is an expensive place to go to college. Fortunately, I was awarded a NASA fellowship that gave me a full ride for thirty-six months. The fellowship came with no stipulations or expectations as to what field I might enter.

I am thankful to the American people for my advanced education, but I have always felt a need to generate some sort of "payback" to show my appreciation. After all, I do not believe the American people paid for my degree to make my life better; they expect something in return, an invention, a new business, or something else. Whether this book will add value to the national discussion on education is yet to be seen, but it is an attempt to settle my assumed debt.

I have many concerns about America's educational system and would like to offer ideas to make improvements. So, I am giving it a try. I have written this book to explain some of my observations about the educational system; it is intended for the public, and I hope it is both engaging and useful.

Acknowledgments

The most important people to thank are the four fourth-grade teachers who volunteered to participate in this study of their school. Without their participation, experience, and good judgment, there would be no book.

Next comes Ms. Nancy Pappas. Nancy retired from the Indiana State Teachers Association and was well versed in the "literature of education." She taught me a great deal about what is going on in that world.

Many thanks to the approximately thirty teachers and former teachers, plus some retired educational executives, who reviewed the original paper; *What's It Like to Teach in a School Graded D?* Their most prevalent comment was that the paper was "spot on."

A special thanks to Mr. Denny Brooks, a retired principal of two schools, who believed the time estimate of sixty-two minutes of lost instruction time was "too low." This bolstered our confidence to keep moving forward.

Franny Gaede, Scholarly Communication librarian—assistant professor in Butler Libraries, was immensely helpful on the website: www.elevateteachers .org. It was Franny who pushed and pushed me to publish something. At first it was going to be a web book, but it matured into a complete book.

Thanks to Jim Shaffer and Steve Cosler of Elevate Indianapolis.

Jeff Rasley was a big help as the first official editor of the manuscript; he became an ardent supporter of this book.

Dr. Chris Edwards liked the ideas presented in the book and recommended it to the publisher, Rowman & Littlefield.

A huge help in both the website and the book is a fellow with the name Chris "The Brain" (Chris Hoyt) and his team of young apprentices. His consulting group is named "Apprenace—We Grow Together." Chris has earned his "stage name" Chris "The Brain" many times over.

Thanks to Janice Minyon, a retired teacher from San Antonio, Texas. Janice taught in the inner city public schools of Houston and successfully dealt with students desperate to learn; students that had been "written off" by the schools.

I have received much help and encouragement from Dr. and Mrs. William Brandt (Bill and Ardis). One of their sons is a high school teacher in St. Paul, MN, so they have a direct experience with the frustrations of the educational system.

Many thanks to my wife, Bonnie Garrett, as she watched me go into yet another learning frenzy over a new topic. She's a sweetheart and did not complain about my time on this project.

Chapter 1

Setting the Scene

DAILY PHONE CALLS

The phone rings. It is late in the afternoon and, as happens many days, it is Son John calling after a day at school; he is on his way home and he needs to talk. In the early part of his sixteen years of teaching career, he did not make these phone calls; these past few years, they've become very regular and, unfortunately, they aren't uplifting calls as he describes what happened in his school that day.

Frustration about not being able to control the classroom or not getting assistance from parents or the administration fuels his discontent. His job is to change lives, and he is not getting enough real teaching time to make much difference in these children's lives. He does not talk about just his fourth-grade classroom but about all the fourth-grade classrooms and often other grades as well.

Today he had to restrain a child going through a tantrum that lasts fourteen minutes.

"Can you actually restrain a child?"

"You can if you do it in the approved way," he says.

He and his colleagues realized that not much happens when you send a disruptive student to the office, so the four fourth-grade teachers developed a plan that takes the main office out of the picture. The teachers deal with discipline issues in their rooms by sending misbehaving students to another one of the fourth-grade rooms.

Imagine working hard to establish a "learning environment" and in pops a teacher with a child he or she could not manage and asks if the student can sit in your class for a while. Or maybe you have a student who is out of control one day, so you simply send him or her to a different classroom for an hour. Is this good discipline?

In another call, he points out that the teachers have lost all their lever-age in terms of benefits they can withhold from misbehaving children. For example, they are not allowed to take away recess—one of the very few remaining options they had. So, the teachers organized misbehaving students into groups who "walk laps" around the play area to use up all the recess time—until a district official saw the students walking laps and chastised the principal for allowing this punishment.

He talks about profane outbursts, students fighting in the middle of a class, and disruptions to group activities to the point that teachers can no longer count on group activities to break the teaching pattern. Phone calls to parents seeking their assistance are often anything but productive. "He's at school; he's your problem." Over time, the bad classroom events relayed in these calls cover a wide range of very *demeaning* and *demoralizing* events for the teachers.

There, the teachers are in a difficult situation, and there is not much they can do about it. They have very little recourse and as adults they wonder why do they have to put up with this environment; as will be shown later, more and more teachers are opting out of teaching.

A teacher like John, with an undergraduate degree in psychology, a degree in elementary education, and a master's degree in psychology, ought to be able to effectively manage his students. In addition, he is a fitness advocate who is about six foot four inches tall and has completed a half iron-man marathon. None of this seems to matter much; in his situation, there are too many factors against him for him to meet his objective of changing lives for the better.

If the events described in these many phone calls are added up, the instruc-tional time for teachers is reduced; this is one of the objectives of this book—to quantify lost instructional time.

WHY BE CONCERNED ABOUT EDUCATIONAL QUALITY?

Any businessman, and most citizens, will have a deep and abiding interest in education. Here are some of the business reasons:

1. Businesses need to hire well-trained people.
2. Our communities need good school systems to attract employees.
3. Just like all other citizens, we want good schools for their own children and grandchildren.
4. We want to see more less-fortunate citizens enjoy the payback for their commitment to education.

5. Most importantly, we are in a major intellectual race with other countries to educate engineers, scientists, and others who hold the keys to innovation and technological advancement.

There Are Many Problems

When sitting on the sidelines, as many do, it is easy to lose track of what is going on in education and delegate the solutions to politicians and educators. Once you get deeply involved, you see many real problems; problems that seem too complicated to solve. This book will speak on these issues. Solutions to many of the problems are not offered, but insights and problem definition help to explain why these difficulties exist. On the other hand, this book does deal head on with one of the big issues facing educators, and practical solutions are presented.

This businessman sees these problems:

1. An educational system that did not improve national reading and math skills in forty-one years.
2. Teachers who are upset about the condition of education and consequently are leaving the profession in even bigger numbers.
3. A looming teacher shortage that will stress our country.
4. An education system that produces "mediocre" students by international standards.
5. A system almost devoid of discipline, and classrooms are full of students who are depriving others of instructional time.
6. A citizenry that is not nearly supportive enough of education in this country.

The Roadmap for This Book

This book begins with an analysis of five major problem areas in the American educational system with comments on the impact the problems have on teachers. This portion of the book is included so that the reader can assess for themselves the condition of the educational system and the impact on teachers and students.

Once through these problem areas, there is one main highway in this book and it is the recognition and quantification of the negative impact that a small number of students have on the education of the balance of their class. Lastly comes the recognition of how these students can be more effectively taught. This main highway has a few interesting diversionary side roads from time to time, but they are all relevant to education and hopefully enlightening for the reader.

Chapter 2

Some Major Issues in Education

Before going any further, time will be spent reviewing some of the hard facts and data on education. One of the biggest reasons education is troubled is because the things done to "fix" it are often based on political motivations and emotions and there is no deep understanding of the real root causes. Just because something sounds good or feels good and has public appeal does not mean it will work. Five major problem areas will be discussed.

A good example of this is the ineffectiveness of incentive pay. The results of two elaborate case studies from Professor Ronald Fryer of Harvard show that incentive pay is not effective (chapter 5). Teachers are motivated by intrinsic values, not extrinsic.

It is proposed that these five problems have, as one of their primary root causes, the lack of character and grit of a small percentage of their students. This lack of character and grit describes the deficiencies that are behind the disruptive student's bad behavior. This relationship will become more apparent and understandable as this book is read.

GOVERNMENT INFLUENCE AND EXPENDITURES—INPUTS AND OUTPUTS

Spending on education is an obviously important issue since most of the expenditures come through local and state governments and are therefore very close to home. It makes up a large portion of local and state budgets. In 2014, the total U.S. expenditure for pre-K to 12 education was $617.6 billion dollars[1]; of this only $52.9 billion (8.6 percent) came from federal sources. The policy influence of the federal government and its bureaucratic workload

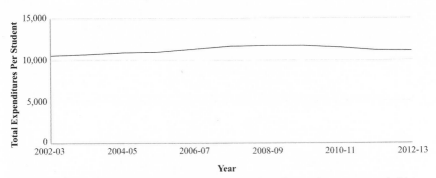

Figure 2.1.   The inflation adjusted spending per student for an eleven-year period.[2]

placed on the local schools is far larger than their contribution to the state and local expenditures.

Figure 2.1 shows the per student expenditure for K-12 after adjustment for inflation. Estimating from the graph, it looks like there has been about a 10 percent real increase in educational expenditures over this eleven-year period. Thus, national expenditures on education are the inputs to a process that are relatively constant; what happened to outputs?

These results come from the National Assessment of Educational Progress (NAEP). NAEP is the largest continuing and nationally representative assessment of what American students know, and can do, in various subjects. NAEP is a congressionally mandated project administered by the National Center for Education Statistics (NCES), within the Institute of Education Sciences (IES) of the U.S. Department of Education.

The first national administration of NAEP exams occurred in 1969. This group is charged with assessing how U.S. students are performing in several different subjects. The most common assessments are in reading and math.

A significant change to state NAEP assessment occurred in 2001 with the reauthorization of the Elementary and Secondary Education Act, also referred to as "No Child Left Behind" legislation. This legislation requires that states that receive Title I funding must participate in state NAEP assessments in mathematics and reading at grades four and eight every two years. State participation in other subjects assessed by state NAEP (science and writing) remains voluntary.

Student Reading and Math Abilities Flat for Forty-One Years

Figure 2.2 is a plot of U.S. student (public and private) reading scores for the time period 1973 to 2012 (forty-one years) for ages nine, thirteen, and

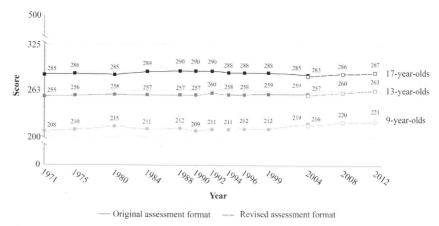

Figure 2.2. Average reading-scale scores on the long-term trend National Assessment of Education Progress (NAEP), by age: selected years 1971–2012.

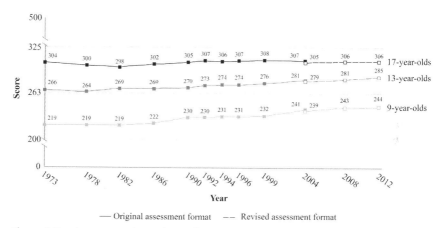

Figure 2.3. Average mathematics-scale scores on the long-term trend National Assessment of Education Progress (NAEP), by age: selected years 1973–2012.

seventeen years. Figure 2.3 is identical in description but it is for math. (A plot of these results is not available for years after 2012.[3]) Note that the maximum score is a 500, and most scores are below 300 or 60 percent.

Statistical analysis reveals that there is a *very slight* improvement in both skills (reading and math) for all age groups except seventeen-year-old readers. But, just because there is a statistically significant upward slope does not mean things are on the mend. If a goal of 65 percent correct answers is set, it takes years, on the current trend lines, to reach that goal. For example, it will take nine-year-olds 304 years to attain 65 percent in reading and 104 years in math. The numbers for thirteen-year-olds are 394 and 76 years; seventeen-year-olds never reach this goal in reading but could reach the math goal in 94 years! By the way, this survey will not be repeated until 2024.

This Was a Period of Intense Governmental Change

Stepping back and looking at the big picture, these "flat" results have persisted during a period of dramatic construction of state and federal bureaucracies, new laws, the creation of many different teaching approaches and assessment exams, attacks on the educational system by the press, and much blame heaped upon teachers.

All this superstructure could well be part of the problem; bureaucracies have a way of creating work that will justify their existence. The teachers complain about all the extra paperwork they must generate to satisfy these requests. Quite obviously extreme corrective action should be attempted, and efforts need to be made to engage the teachers in the solutions.

The Country Has a Major Systemic Problem

Here is a process with relatively flat inputs and flat outputs. The question is why? Poor results like these do not occur with spot problems here and there; the problem is systemic throughout most of the country and in most of our schools.

This book quickly dispenses with the issue of intellectual capability. Teachers say that almost all their students have the intellectual capabilities to pass assessment exams, and in chapter 4, data is presented that supports this contention.

Is the lack of real expenditure increases the root cause of the flat test score performance? There is serious doubt that money is a primary root cause of this lack luster performance. Is it a long line of incompetent teachers— plausible but highly unlikely? The problem lies much deeper, it is cultural; America just doesn't give education the importance it deserves or it receives in many other countries.

The American public routinely ignores stories coming out of the classrooms of students swearing at their teachers, student belligerence, and even hostility. This type of behavior is attributed to ineffective teaching that does not "engage" the students. As will be seen later, some of these students are unmanageable by all but a handful of teachers. The teachers never seem to get a break because the way the press presents their case puts the teachers in the spotlight; the provoking actions of the students are never an issue.

INTERNATIONAL COMPARISONS— WHY SUCH A POOR SHOWING?

Before delving into how American students measure up, position this topic as a person-to-person competition with students from around the world to gain perspective on the importance of this topic.

Education Is an International Competition for Our Future

To better understand the nature of international education competition, think about a time trial in the Tour de France bicycle race. This is a race against the clock, the riders never see a competitor. Think of the discipline that the riders must have to go "all out" without the motivation of a competitor either in front or in back. Where do they draw the tenacity to ride for kilometers to finish up number one? They have certainly trained hard and know very well what they must do to finish high in the order.

International educational performance is much like a time trial. American students are in a competition where they cannot see their competitor. It is indeed a race because if the U.S. students do not finish high in the order, this country, as a nation, loses the race and, for the most part, never knows the competitor. Losing the race does not have immediate consequences, but the persistent losses become a part of a long-term economic slide where wealth slowly moves from U.S. workers to "winners" throughout the world. Students in China, South Korea, Singapore, and India, just to name a few, are working harder, attending classes for more hours each day and more days a year.

Do they worry about the competition from the United States? They probably do, but when their instructors tell them how complacent U.S. students have become, they realize they are winning the race—a race that most American students never realize is even happening.

Where Do U.S. Students Stand?

One way to begin this part is to research and report on how our students stack up to students in other countries. As the reading began, this approach proved unproductive because U.S. international rankings, near the middle of the pack, are well known, and there is *little that can be said* to make the picture brighter. The United States has a large and diverse student population, and when all segments are included—as well they should be, to reflect the nature of the country's citizens—the United States is in the middle of the pack.

Digging deeper into this area of research reveals the real root cause. Do Americans truly value education? Not enough do.

Here is material from the *Daily Beast* that is "spot on":[4]

For all our national hand-wringing about standardized testing and teacher ten-
ure, many of us immersed in the American education debate can't escape the
nagging suspicion that something else—something cultural, something nearly
intangible—is holding back our school system. In 1962, historian Richard Hofstadter famously dubbed it "anti-intellectualism in American life.

"A host of educational problems has arisen from indifference," he wrote,
"underpaid teachers, overcrowded classrooms, double-schedule schools, broken-
down school buildings, inadequate facilities and a number of other failings
that come from something else—the cult of athleticism, marching bands, high-
school drum majorettes, ethnic ghetto schools, de-intellectualized curricula,
the failure to educate in serious subjects, the neglect of academically gifted
children."

It would be comforting to think that since Hofstadter's time a string of
national reform initiatives—A Nation at Risk, No Child Left Behind, Race to
the Top, the Common Core—has addressed these issues. And though there has
been some progress on the margins, journalist Amanda Ripley is here with a
riveting new book, *The Smartest Kids in the World*, to show us exactly why,
compared with many of their peers in Europe and Asia, American students are
still performing below the mark. According to the OECD, 20 countries have
higher high school graduation rates than the United States. Among developed
nations, our children rank 17th in reading and 31st in math. Even Poland, with
high child poverty rates like our own, boasts stronger student achievement and
faster system-wide improvement.

Here is a similar opinion from a website: Building Bridges between
Schools and Parent—this quotation is written like an editorial and no author
is listed:[5]

National Rankings Show American Schools Lower: It's Not Because of Bad
Teachers
    Why Does the U.S.A. Fall Behind in Education?

Studies suggest that national culture differences account for why some countries rank more highly on education than other countries. That's a hard thing
to change. How do you get an entire culture, for example, to start valuing
education?

The studies suggest the answer lies, not with teacher pay, not with the quality of teachers (although that's certainly part of it), but with a much broader,
and problematic issue. National culture (the beliefs, values of the country).

The countries that fare better than the USA on these metrics simply have
cultures that value education more highly. They also tend to have cultures
that tend to be less individualistic and value the welfare of the "group"

whether it be family, neighborhood, organization, and much less on individual accomplishment, and "standing out." In countries that fare better, teachers are more respected and held in higher esteem.

The reality is you can take all the best teachers in the world, and put upon them all the demands placed on American teachers that result from the American culture, and you counteract any benefits you might get from a more motivated and skilled teaching force. Maybe we as members of society, and parents should look in the mirror before we complain about how our schools are "failing" our children.

Based on research, these citations seem accurate. Many U.S. universities had active programs to recruit students from all over the world. Students from Singapore, India, China, Taiwan, Korea, and others were deadly serious about their studies. These students really care about education, and they have a passion for learning. This attitude was not particularly prevalent in the American students at Indiana University—though, in general, the quality of most of the students was acceptable. However, many of the American students seemed easily distracted from their studies and did not show "a love of learning."

THE TEACHING PROFESSION IN PERIL

Encounters with teachers of low-income students are generally very disturbing. They have made a commitment to spend their lives changing others for the better, but this is not what's happening. They are the ones changing, growing cynical, looking for a way out, seeking early retirement, or just quitting outright. Meanwhile the kids just keep on moving on to higher-grade levels without changing their behavior.

In a recent interview with a successful high school principal here in Indianapolis, they pointed out that they recommend that students do not go into teaching, "No money and you have to put up with a lot of frustration."

The teaching profession in the United States is suffering from many negative influences. As the evidence, summarized below shows, here are some of the issues:

1. Low teacher morale
2. Poor teacher retention
3. Enrollment in many of the countries' schools of education is dropping—this will lead to a teacher shortage
4. Low teacher status

Each of these issues will be addressed in sequence.

LOW TEACHER MORALE

The Metropolitan Life Insurance Company began a survey of teachers and then principals around 1984 and continued until 2012. For some unknown reason, they produced no reports after 2012. Here is an excerpt from the 2012 report:[6] "The 2012 MetLife Survey of Teachers found that teacher job satisfaction declined from 62 percent of teachers feeling 'very satisfied' in 2008 to 39 percent by 2012. This was the lowest in the 25-year history of the survey." "Half (51%) of teachers report feeling under great stress several days a week, an increase of 15 percentage points over 36% of teachers reporting that level in 1985."

Newsweek reports on a series of teaching issues in a 2015 article entitled: *Why Has Teacher Morale Plummeted?*[7] "Over the past few decades, teacher professionalism and morale declined as education was turned into a market with a push for high-stakes testing and a centralized control of education."

About Education[8] points out that teacher morale is declining throughout the United States. The main contributors are teacher criticism, low pay, testing pressure, and unruly students. These declining attitudes are forcing administrators to make deliberate plans to boost teacher morale.

From *The Atlantic*, 2012,[9] "It's not a simple matter of burnout. Kids who come to school hungry—and parents who don't care—also weigh heavily on educators."

POOR TEACHER RETENTION

This comes from Owen Phillips from nprED[10]

Every year, thousands of fresh-faced teachers are handed the keys to a new classroom, given a pat on the back and told, "Good luck!"

Over the next five years, though, nearly half of those teachers will transfer to a new school or leave the profession altogether—only to be replaced with similarly fresh-faced teachers.

We've been reporting this month on the pipeline into teaching—and hearing from teachers themselves about why they stay.

Richard Ingersoll, who has studied the issue for years, says there's a revolving door of teacher turnover that costs school districts upwards of $2.2 billion a year.

But most of the turnover is driven by school conditions. Salary is not the main thing. It's important, but not the main thing. And that's an important finding because the teaching force is so large—it's now America's largest occupation—that raising everyone's salaries is a very expensive proposition.[11]

What else is highly correlated with the decision to stay or leave?[12]

A whole other big one that always rises to the top is student misbehavior and discipline. But there's an interesting thing in the data, which is that the amount of student behavior and discipline problems varies dramatically between schools. And poverty is by no means the only, or main factor. And some schools do a far better job of dealing with it, coping with it and addressing it than other schools. And those schools that do a better job of coping with it have significantly better teacher retention. We have this finding that schools can manage behavioral issues in good ways or bad ways.

This quotation makes a point that has not been emphasized yet in this book. Many schools in low-income areas do just fine with discipline. As will be seen in chapter 4, 114 high-poverty schools in Indiana are graded A. There are many factors that determine the level of discipline; basically, it gets down to the will of the leadership and support from their management.

THE CRISIS IN TEACHER SUPPLY

On February 29, 2016, Dr. John Jacobson, dean and professor at the Teachers College, Ball State University, Muncie, Indiana, spoke at the Indianapolis Scientech Club. His topic was *The State of Teacher Supply*. His opening slide was: "Where have all the teachers gone?" He then pointed out that declining enrollment in teacher preparation is a national trend. His warning:

TEXT BOX 2.1

A teacher shortage is just the beginning of a huge workforce development problem if not corrected.

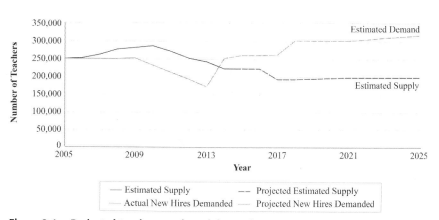

Figure 2.4.   Projected teacher supply and demand.

In September of 2016, the Learning Policy Institute published a comprehensive report titled: *A Coming Crisis in Teaching? Teacher Supply, Demand, and Shortages in the U.S.*[13] This is an excellent report, and the coming teacher shortage can effectively be described from its executive summary. This graph tells the story in one look.

Figure 2.4 says that in 2018, there will be a shortfall of approximately 112,000 teachers. Since the demand for teachers in 2018 is approximately 300,000, this is a 37 percent shortfall. This level of shortfall will be at least this large until 2021. Here are the four factors behind these shortages:

1. A decline in teacher preparation enrollments
2. District efforts to return to prerecession pupil to teacher ratios
3. Increased student enrollment
4. High teacher attrition

Each point is discussed:

Decline in teacher preparation: Between 2009 and 2014, teacher education enrollments *dropped* from 691,000 to 451,000—a 35 percent reduction. This amounts to a 240,000 reduction in the graduation of professional teachers in the year 2014 as compared to 2009.

After the 2008–2009 recession, pupil-teachers ratio rose to 16:1; to return to the prerecession level of 15.3:1 will require hiring an additional 145,000 teachers.

Student enrollments have been relatively flat for the past decade but the National Center for Educational Statistics predicts that student enrollment *will increase* approximately three million students in the coming decade.

Teacher attrition is estimated to be approximately 8 percent per year— these departing teachers are the largest producer of new teacher demand.

WHY ARE TEACHERS LEAVING THE PROFESSION?

The annual loss of teachers is driven by factors other than retirement. Only about one-third of those leaving in each year are retiring. Dissatisfaction is the primary driver of the volunteer departures. In other words, 67 percent of the openings are created by unhappy teachers. This book deals with what is one of the primary forces of dissatisfaction and that is student behavior. (This is a supposition and not a conclusion of the report cited above.) The report's reasons are:

1. Concerns with the administration ranging from lack of support, lack of control, to no input over teaching decisions

2. Testing and accountability pressures
3. Dissatisfaction with a teaching career
4. Unhappiness with various working conditions

Note that pay is not a listed reason for departure. Though salaries are a concern, the typical teacher is in the profession for intrinsic reasons—they want to change lives and want to have an impact on a child's future.

From Ed News Daily,[14]

Many teachers are experiencing teacher burnout within five years. Institutions across America are dealing with rapid changes, new teaching demands, the Common Core, shocking assessment policies, and levels of technology not seen in years. Taking a look at the big data for this site specifically, the four most common phrases typed in via Google that bring teachers to this site are:

—Why did I become a teacher
—Companies that hire teachers
—How teachers can make more money
—Teacher burnout

Unhappy Teachers Produce Unhappy Students

The picture of unhappy teachers is becoming clearer, and more discouraging news is yet to come. Throughout the nation, many teachers (mostly public-school teachers) are unhappy. There has always been significant turnover in the early teacher ranks, but it is now accelerating. What is more disturbing is the decline in students wanting to become teachers. This means that we're not growing our "seed corn" thereby leading to major crop shortages in the future.

There are teachers all over America who are discouraged and unmotivated; they project an attitude that will affect their students who then suffer in both academic and nonacademic ways. For these issues, numbers, statistics, blue ribbons and test scores deem themselves meaningless and do not provide a true picture of what is taking place daily across classrooms in America. If teachers do not want to be in the classroom, it is only natural for students to feel this resentment and displaced animosity. Read the inserted box below to better understand nonverbal communication and its role in the classroom.

This situation begs to ask a question: why would students want to be in the classroom if their teachers do not want to be there? Teachers set the tone, the mood, and deliver the expectations in the classroom daily. From the minute kids walk into the classroom, the energy and attitude transmitted from the teacher sets the mood of the day, either positive or negative.

TEXT BOX 2.2   NONVERBAL COMMUNICATION

There is some early research (1960s) that states that the actual words that come out of our mouths comprise only 7 percent of the communication between people. There is strong disagreement to this very low number, but one thing is for sure—voice tone and body language are very important. The nonverbals include the use of visual clues such as body language, distance, physical environments/appearance, and even touch. It can also include the use of time and eye contact, the actions of looking while talking and listening, frequency of glances, patterns of fixation, pupil dilation, and blink rate.

The lesson to be learned is this—if a teacher is upset with his or her job, it will be very difficult to hide this from the students. It may be possible in the early morning but doubtful for an entire day.

Why Do Teachers Leave Their Profession

There is a lot of movement within and departing their profession. Here's a comment from the literature:[15]

> What do we know about why some teachers stay in the profession and why some don't? We don't have a lot of research on the decision to stay or not. But we have a lot of data on the flip side: why teachers move to other schools or leave the profession. For example, beginning teachers are more likely to drop out. Those from top colleges—the most selective colleges and universities—are more likely to drop out. And we know that minority teachers are more likely to drop out than white, non-Hispanic teachers.

WHAT HAPPENED TO DISCIPLINE?

For reasons that are beyond comprehension, many of today's school systems have either backed off or forsaken discipline. Part of this is due to the presence of *disruptive* students (see chapter 4) and their difficulty to control. They are particularly tough to manage by most of the commonly used approaches and by most teachers.

As education is discussed with friends, teachers, and former teachers, almost all of them say, "The kids are terrible these days." Later this book will quantify, for one school, that an average of six students are disruptive per class. Are all kids "really terrible" these days? Some are, but the vast majority (77 percent) of the study school's students are "just fine."

The Concept of Self-Regulation

An ideal classroom would be made up of *engaged* students (defined in chapter 4). In the literature of modern psychology, these students have good self-regulation skills. (Perhaps in another time, they would have good "self-control.") Cybele Raver[16] is a psychology professor from New York University and has written extensively on this concept. Be aware that much of her research was done on pre-K students; many of whom were studied in the Chicago School Readiness Project (CSPR). It is believed that these finding will also be useful in the early grades of school.

Self-regulation is defined as the self-management of attention, emotion, and brain executive functions for the attainment of a goal. There is an abundance of research that points to the ways in which children who are exposed to the chronic environmental stresses associated with low income reduce their ability to self-regulate, leading to negative outcomes in their behavior and higher-order cognitive skills.

Here is the good news. The poor children's behavior and mental skills are relatively malleable or plastic in the face of changing environmental conditions. *In plain English, this means that there is the possibility of a reversal of the adverse consequences of poverty.*

One of the keys to success is a teacher who is properly trained in rewarding positive behavior and redirecting negative behavior. The results of the CSRP show that teachers properly trained in activities that promote self-regulation were significantly more successful in providing more emotionally and behaviorally supportive classrooms than teachers who were not so trained.

This classroom-based intervention also led to clear reductions in the children's emotional and behavioral difficulties. These changes come about in classrooms that have more structure, clear routines, and fewer episodes where teachers and students find themselves in conflict or coercive interaction.

A school's disciplinary philosophy should be aimed at reinforcing the idea that the student's behavior and mental skills are relatively malleable or plastic in the face of changing environmental conditions. It should produce an environment that fosters self-regulation rather than destroying it.

Here is information from a Public Agenda national study that will be described in chapter 4.[17]

It is almost unanimously accepted among teachers (97%) that school needs good discipline and behavior in order to flourish, and 78% of parents agree.

It is also widely accepted among both groups that part of a school's mission—in addition to teaching the 3 R's is to teach kids to follow rules so they can become productive citizens (93% and 88%).

Lastly, also from the Public Agenda paper:

> More than 1 in 3 teachers say they have seriously considered quitting the profession—or know a colleague who has left—because student discipline and behavior became so intolerant. And 85% believe new teachers are particularly unprepared for dealing with behavior problems.

Lessons Are Being Learned

The one quotation above refers to the school's responsibility to teach the children to be productive citizens—this means they must be sensitive to rules and able to follow them when needed. *Do not forget that behavioral lessons are being learned no matter what is done.*

Without discipline, the lesson being taught is that it's okay to swear at a teacher or fight in school since nothing bad ever happens. Students think it must be okay, so they will keep on doing it. On the other hand, if swearing is the issue and mild rebukes and pep talks begin at an early age and are consistently carried forward as the students progress, the problem will be managed because they have learned what not to do.

Be a Coach, Not a Judge Issuing Punishment

In a successful environment, discipline would be treated as a coaching experience as opposed to judgment and punishment. This makes it a meaningful learning experience and strengthens self-regulation skills. Children want to be respected but need help learning about what is the right way to behave.

To be effective, the discipline must start early and be consistently applied throughout the student's school years. Hear from Paul Tough:[18]

> This doesn't mean, of course, that teachers should excuse or ignore bad behavior in the classroom. But it does explain why harsh punishments so often prove to be ineffective over the long term in motivating troubled children to succeed. And it suggests that school-discipline programs might be more effective if they were to focus less on imposing punishment and more on creating a classroom environment in which students who lack self-regulatory capacities can find the tools and context they need to develop them.

Here's a story from *NEA Today* to illustrate the benefits of positive interventions.[19]

> Meet Lynn Harrison of Redland Middle School in Montgomery County, MD. You know you're onto something good when your school goes from referring over 1200 students to the principal's office to under 30 in just one year.

"As a staff, we were thrilled at the respect that was growing in our building," says Harrison, coordinator of Redland's Positive Behavior Intervention Strategies (PBIS) program.

The PBIS process emphasizes constructive interventions as an alternative to punitive discipline. Redland, a bright, airy middle school with students who look like they're happy to be there, has won an award for its efforts every year since starting the program in 2009. Equally impressive, Redland's referral rates broken down by student ethnicity are pretty evenly distributed among white, black, and Hispanic students—unlike some schools that improve their overall numbers but still show disproportionate referral and suspension rates for students of color.

Implement school wide expectations and teach positive behaviors. Once we determined our core expectation and school motto—Respect School, Self, and Others—we set behavioral expectations for the classroom, hallway, buses, and cafeteria and posted these throughout the building and in all classrooms. Staff and students are taught the expectations through modeling, and lessons throughout the year reinforce these expectations. Even our announcements end with our school motto.

The Oaks Academy of Indianapolis has a policy that requires 50 percent of their students come from low-income families. Discipline issues are well managed. They have only asked a small handful of students to leave since they began in 1998. Meanwhile, their enrollment has increased from 53 (1998) students to 732 (2016). For this school, discipline is not a concern because their eleven good habits and great teachers keep it under control.

Here is the other side of the coin—families are suing school systems to assure that they have peaceful and effective classrooms in which their children can be educated. The public should file more lawsuits like this one. This is just one way, of several, to advocate for any action that will allow students amenable to learning, to have a great learning experience. Here is one of these cases:

Class Lawsuit filed against City Ed Department for failing to protect students from violence in schools.[20]

Eleven students and ten parents have reached the breaking point on the New York City schools allowing violence to disrupt their schools and endanger their children. All these students have related compelling stories of abuse to substantiate their claims.

They have filed a lawsuit with the U.S. District Court for the Eastern District of New York. This is the first-ever class action on school safety in New York State, and it seeks to hold the New York City Department of Education accountable for depriving students of their constitutionally protected right to a public education by failing to address in-school violence committed by students and teachers.

Their claim is that the New York schools have deprived their children of their constitutional right to a violence-free school. They are not seeking punitive damages but only want the schools to live up to their own rules.

Why Is Discipline so Important to the Success of a Student?

Six years of mentoring seniors at a large Indianapolis public high school has been revealing. The mentoring task was to assist the students through their senior year and into college. Mentoring these students created a real appreciation for these kids and a respect for the way they dealt with their issues. One student was "kicked out" of the family apartment because there was no longer room for her. She stayed with the families of various friends over the entire school year. Generally, she handled her situation quite well.

The biggest issue faced by the team of mentors was getting the students to keep their appointments. Multiple e-mails would be sent to students to set up an appointment in the school library for 7:30 a.m. on an agreed-upon morning, right after they arrived at school. They would send an e-mail back saying they understood the appointment time and that they would be there. Repeatedly they did not show up for the appointment, this behavior was true for the other mentors as well. The last student mentoree failed to show up three times in a row. This ended a six-year mentoring experience.

This inability to self-manage shows a serious lack of self-discipline. Without good discipline, students are going to have troubles showing up for job interviews and showing up for work on a regular schedule basis. If they cannot handle criticism, they will sooner or later butt heads with their bosses, and they will lose the battle. If they cannot manage conflict, they will face confrontations with fellow workers, bosses, and probably, customers. Without self-discipline, they will not improve their job skills and will get stuck at a low-level job. This is why school discipline is so important to their future lives.

Learning self-discipline falls into the character and grit side of the success equation (chapter 3). It is an essential skill for the success of a student.

UNEMPOWERED TEACHERS

The first step in the Total Quality process is: *If you want to understand and improve a job, ask the people who do the job.* Asking employees to improve their organizations will engage more employee brains in the pursuit of better outcomes. Psychologically, it is very rewarding and empowering to be acting as part of the management process of the company.

It is motivating to have a say in what happens in your organization.

Consider the profession of teaching. In all candor, teachers are a group of professionals who are probably the least empowered of all professions. They are told what to teach, when to teach, and how to teach it. Common Core certainly accelerated this point to the extreme. Their teaching loads keep increasing as school administrators keep adding more and more initiatives. They get blamed for most of the bad things happening in education and get very little credit for many of the good things that occur. Administrators often speak for the teachers but seldom speak to them. Is it a surprise that there is a morale problem, especially when a large number of unmanageable students are added to the mix?

TEXT BOX 2.3

Administrators often speak for the teachers but seldom speak to them.

Teacher unions have damaged the profession over time and enhanced poor management-labor relations. The teacher's unions seemed very self-serving over the years and developed extreme political power due to their numbers, funding, organizational capabilities, and close association. Why didn't the unions lobby and even strike over the conditions in their classrooms? Fighting for classroom conditions would have been a win-win outcome.

In many cases, teachers are sent into classrooms where their chances of being successful are very low. This leads to rapid burnout, losses to the profession, and the building of a bad reputation for the teaching profession. Most importantly, they are not fulfilling a teacher's basic mission—to educate.

Listen to what Paul M. Terry of the University of Memphis says:[21]

Empowerment, also referred to as shared decision-making, is essential to school reform and to the changing demands in a global world. The principal is the building leader who structures the climate to empower both teachers and students at the site. Empowerment translates into teacher leadership and exemplifies a paradigm shift with the decisions made by those working most closely with students rather than those at the top of the pyramid.

This is from nprED[22]

What are some of the important factors driving the decision to stay or leave?
One of the main factors is the issue of voice, and having say, and being able to have input into the key decisions in the building that affect a teacher's job. This is something that is a hallmark of professions. It's something that teachers usually have very little of, but it does vary across schools and it's very highly correlated with the decision whether to stay or leave.

I've worked with these data a lot going back last couple of decades. Where nationally, large samples of teachers are asked, "How much say does the faculty collectively have?" And, "How much leeway do you have in your classroom over a series of issues?" It turns out both levels are important for decisions whether to stay or to part. And what's interesting about this finding [is that] this would not cost money to fix. This is an issue of management.

School bureaucracies have a very self-serving reputation. The typical teacher strategy is to "not make waves," a characteristic of many bureaucracies. One of a bureaucracy's goals is to perpetuate itself at all costs. Any threat to the bureaucracy is a threat to each person in it. In addition, bureaucratic organizations offer cover from responsibility since groups make decisions. A businessman views a bureaucracy as overhead; a bureaucrat sees it as power. The more people managed, the more money made.

TEXT BOX 2.4

A businessman views a bureaucracy as overhead; a bureaucrat sees it as power. The more people managed, the more money made.

What schools must do is to ask their teachers how to improve their jobs. They know what is best for the students, how they would like to be managed, and how they should teach the material. To make this successful, the administration must seriously consider their proposals. If the teachers need to better understand some of the constraints faced by the administration, these should be explained, and the teachers figure ways to "stay within the rules" and still be successful. The teachers need to feel empowered, and this is what it is going to take—they need to have a bigger say in what happens in their classrooms.

Here are a few observations on three of the key administrative players in school administration.

The Principal

The school principal is the most important position in the school system. A principal sets the tone, hires and motivates the teachers, and takes personal responsibility for the results. He or she is directly involved with the teachers and the students. A principal determines approaches, ideally with the help of the teachers, to get the students and parents involved. He or she is the key to success—this is where the best talent should go!

The Superintendent

The superintendent is the leader of large bureaucracy. Generally, he or she walks down a difficult road as he or she attempts to please many factions. Look at how some deal with poor performance. A superintendent can't blame the school board, because they are the boss. He or she can't blame the bureaucracy since that would be self-incriminating. He or she can't blame the parents since they would complain to the school board.

As was already discussed, a superintendent can't blame the students because that will be seen as a "cop-out" and could light a huge political fire. The only people left are the teachers. Despite the removal of discipline by the school boards, violence in the classrooms, many *disruptive* students, and sometimes weak leadership from the school's administration, the teachers are still responsible for the poor performance. The real responsibility for poor performance goes well beyond the teachers.

The School Board

School board—as signs say on some executive desks, "The Buck Stops Here." This is certainly true for a school board. They are the board of directors of their local educational organization; they have responsibility for it all. They have a difficult task, especially with all the recent funding restraints. Their primary mission is to educate their area's children.

One retired superintendent commented that, generally, school boards are focused on providing opportunities and improvements for children like their own. They are the ones who keep on piling new initiatives on the teachers. Do they ever talk directly to the teachers and ask them about their workloads, teaching conditions, support from their management, and other things that will allow the board to better meet their mission of educating children? Generally, the school board members *are too responsive to parental complaints and not responsive enough to teacher complaints.*

Parental Complaints Top Years of Experience

A few years ago, while I was tearing down a display from a Boy Scout Pow Wow at a Marion County (Indianapolis) eastside high school, a school policeman was watching. How long he had worked at this school? Thirty-four years, he said. Do you still have faith in our kids? I asked. The kids were okay, he said, but not the parents. He said that some of the parents are just awful. He must be careful they don't file a complaint against him.

For example, recently one of the parents stopped right in the middle of the road by the school to let the kids out; she blocked traffic in both directions.

He should have asked her to go to the usual drop off location but didn't because he was afraid she would file a complaint against him and get him in trouble. Thirty-four years with the school, and he'll get into trouble for doing his job! That is not supportive management; parents hold sway over the school administrations far out of proportion to what it should be.

What are others saying? The quotations presented below make it clear that there is not universal support for school boards; this is a manifestation of the fact that "The Buck Stops Here" is not working. Why are the school boards letting us down with such poor school performance?

From the *American School Board Journal*[23] (Here they are repeating what other publications are saying about school boards—they later try to rebut these arguments.)

> It's time to "kill all the school boards," proposed a 2008 article in The Atlantic, which claimed that "local control has become a disaster for our schools." School boards are "a governance system that is too often ineffective, if not dysfunctional," suggested a 2009 Education Week special report. And "local control . . . needs a makeover," concluded the Fordham Institute earlier this year, when it promised a three-year effort "to put governance at the center of the education-reform conversation.

One area of school board control that is being ignored in some districts is school discipline. The board bears the ultimate responsibility for discipline in the classroom, but many boards have taken a pass on discipline.

Discipline is a win-win proposition, the kids win because they develop self-control and respect, the learning environment in the classrooms is much improved, and teacher morale goes way up. Why is this so hard to see? Data shows that teachers and the general public strongly support discipline in our schools. The school boards must receive parental complaints or perhaps even threats of lawsuits because of discipline issues. If this is the case, schools should lobby legislatures for relief.

Some years ago, family members hosted exchange students. One student was a bright young lady from Russia and more recently another was an exceptional young lady from Vietnam. Both students were astounded by the lack of respect shown to their American teachers by the students. It was so far from the reality of their schools at home that they just could not understand it, and why it was tolerated. This feedback is consistent with criticism of the U.S. attitude about education—the public tolerates and sometimes fosters this lack of respect.

Chapter 3

What Children Need to Succeed

The last chapter focused on some of the major issues in education. From this point on in the book, emphasis will be shifted to laying the groundwork of some of the changes that will help to resolve some of the problems discussed in the prior chapter. Two of the following sections (Hope and Success) illuminate the ingredients for student success. By developing an understanding of what makes a student successful, then setting up an environment that will offer the missing elements, a number of the problems discussed above will be impacted; in some cases, the impact will be dramatic.

HOPE—THE PREREQUISITE FOR SUCCESS

Steve Cosler and Jim Shaffer, knowledgeable men who work within schools to alleviate the effects of poverty on the education of children, point out that the perquisite for any success with children resides in their level of hope. Without hope, nothing good happens.

Steve Cosler is a cofounder and chairman of the board, and Jim Shaffer is another cofounder and chief executive officer of Elevate Indianapolis.[1] Their focus is on creating hope in high school students and teaching them some of the elements of character and grit.

This section of the book will investigate hope and the role it plays in the lives of children. A conceptual model will be proposed that will allow visualization and discussion of the topic. Many low-income children face situations that can destroy hope thereby making the "success equation" irrelevant. The "success equation" is discussed in the next section of the book. What really matters are ways to either keep hope alive or restore it if diminished. There are things that can be done to preserve and restore hope.

Discussion on Hope

Here are operational definitions of hope:

Definitions of hope

- Dictionary—a feeling of expectation and desire for a certain thing to happen
- The ability and clarity to see a path to a goal or better future.

Here are some thoughts on Hope from Steve Cosler.[2] Based on their environment, poor children only see the path of their family and friends—which is, most often, not good. Someone must help identify his or her strengths, passions, and God-given skills and turn them into a vision then a path. Want to be an accountant and have the aptitude? Take more math, graduate from high school, go to college, graduate in accounting, get a CPA. Show me people, like me, who have made it. Harder than it sounds but that's the idea. We often quote former surgeon general Dr. Del Elliott "In order to have a chance at a productive life, a child must have at least one adult relationship that is positive, caring and long-term."

A Picture of Hope

The level of hope for a child depends upon several things, such as age, their environment, parenting, and so on. Not every poor child suffers from a loss of hope but for those that do, here is a graphical portrayal of what hope looks like.

Figure 3.1 illustrates that children begin to conceptualize their world through TV viewing, travel, and so on at around three years old. At this point hope is

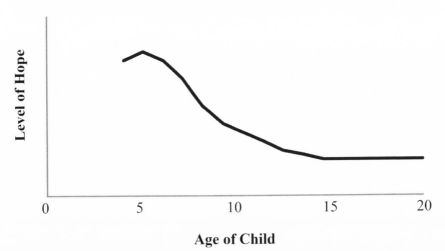

Age of Child

Figure 3.1.   The picture of hope for some poor children.

beginning to build in a positive way. Building continues until age five to six years and then the reality of the family's situation begins to decline, creating the downward slope of the hope curve. The creation of this curve is the consensus picture drawn after discussions with several experts on child poverty.

As the children age, the slope continues downward then begins to level off as they are forced to accept their reality and see no recourse out of their situation. One expert believes that after age eighteen, it is very difficult to move the curve up; others believe it can happen at any age.

This loss of hope brings to mind Geoffrey Canada's anguished comment in the movie *Waiting for Superman*. Once his mother told him the truth that superman was only a comic book hero, he was shattered. If superman was dead, who was going to come and save them from their terribly difficult life? This certainly dropped his hope level.

PREVENTING THE DECLINE IN HOPE

What activities, events, interventions, and so on must be employed to keep, or minimize, the decline from occurring?

Here are some of the things that are necessary for a successful intervention with the poor child who need to be uplifted. It is difficult to say that all are needed, but certainly most of them will lead to a more positive outcome. One thing for sure—not much happens without caring adults.

1. At least one caring adult; several would be better
2. Must be able to develop a positive image of their future
3. Must develop competency in school subjects

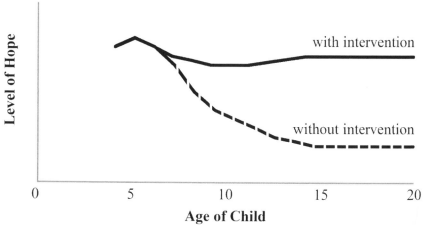

Figure 3.2. The picture of hope for poor children with intervention at age eight.

4. Must have food and physical security
5. Must develop emotional balance and control
6. If religious, must develop a spiritual belief system

Figure 3.2 is a picture of the curve after successful intervention around the age of eight. The dotted line is the path of hope without intervention.

A Key Idea

One of the experts who helped to craft the hope graph is Reverend Jay Height, executive director of the Shepherd Community Center in Indianapolis. The Center's mission is to *break the cycle of multigenerational poverty*. Here is a key piece of advice from Reverend Height:

TEXT BOX 3.1

Programs don't work, people do. Relationships with caring adults are essential for success.

Without a significant intervention by caring adults, there will be no positive and meaningful change for children in poverty. This does not exclude parents, if they are caring adults. Generally, this is why making handouts to families in poverty will not help the child if good parenting is lacking. These children need caring adults in their lives. These could be volunteer tutors, a quality day care, mentors, and so on. Just handing out money does not lead to lasting results.

What they have also learned is that there needs to be something given in return for benefitting from a program. As they deal with people entrapped in multigenerational poverty, they might ask for a payment of $3.00 for a bag of groceries, $2.00 for school supplies, and so on. The "cost" to the recipient does not have to be large but outright gifting creates, in the longer term, a bad attitude from the recipient. Without some sort of participation on their part, dependency sets in, and hope diminishes for the family.

Situational poverty, a house fire, homelessness, and the like are not treated this way; the people need immediate free assistance. It is only after multiple gifting that dependence is created, and this is an inappropriate application of relief.

Aiming too high can destroy hope—Figure 3.3 is a diagram of the Maslovian Hierarchy of Needs:

Many years ago, the RAND Corporation produced a report that discussed the Maslovian hierarchy and how, over time, U.S. citizens were moving

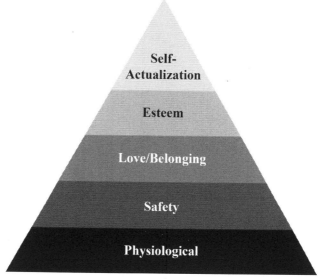

Figure 3.3. Maslovian hierarchy of needs.

toward self-actualization. The report pointed out how difficult it is for a person to advance up the pyramid more than one or two levels in one generation. The bottom levels are about food and shelter security; many poor children are in this base level.

Alternative Paths for Their Futures

The current educational philosophy, for Indiana, is aimed at preparing all students to someday attend a university. The state assessment exam, ISTEP[3], is designed and administered in this way. There should be another path for children, and it should begin at an early age.

Looking back at the list of things necessary to successfully intervene and elevate hope, one item is that it must be able to develop a positive image of their future. They are in a family that has almost no history of steady employment, high school or college, and suddenly they are going to attempt to see themselves as a university graduate. This may be so out of reach in their minds that, in futility, they give up.

Being a university graduate, both for financial and intellectual reasons, is a real stretch for many disadvantaged students but many can imagine themselves as a plumber, electrician, auto transmission expert, medical technician, and so on. Indeed, some will be able to make the leap to a university future but for many, this is too much of a jump. It would be better to offer a fork in the road with the two branches: one leading to a college preparatory path and the other to a skilled trade. There must always be a path back to the university tract if the student has the ability to make the move.

Here's an article from Forbes[4] written by Nicholas Wyman that supports a two-track design: *Why We Desperately Need to Bring Back Vocational Training in Schools.*

For many years, the U.S. educational system taught vocational skills as well as the usual school topics of English, math, and so on. In the 1950s, the idea of separating the students into those that would probably go to college from those more likely to end up in the vocational work force grew in popularity.

This separation fostered the belief by some that the real criteria for the division of students were not aptitude but socioeconomic level or race. By the end of the 1950s, what was previously a respectable course of action turned repugnant for many working-class families and families of color.

The resolution of this split of the students did not bring vocational training back into the academic core; instead the idea evolved that all students should be prepared to attend college.

So, what's the harm in prepping kids for college? Won't all students benefit from a high-level, four-year academic degree program? As it turns out, not really. For one thing, people have a huge and diverse range of different skills and learning styles. Not everyone is good at math, biology, history and other traditional subjects that characterize college-level work. Not everyone is fascinated by Greek mythology, or enamored with Victorian literature, or enraptured by classical music. Some students are mechanical; others are artistic. Some focus best in a lecture hall or classroom; still others learn best by doing, and would thrive in the studio, workshop or shop floor.

And not everyone goes to college. The latest figures from the U.S. Bureau of Labor Statistics (BLS) show that about 68% of high school students attend college. That means over 30% graduate with neither academic nor job skills.

But even the 68% aren't doing so well. Almost 40% of students who begin four-year college programs don't complete them, which translates into a whole lot of wasted time, wasted money, and burdensome student loan debt. Of those who do finish college, one-third or more will end up in jobs they could have had without a four-year degree. The BLS found that 37% of currently employed college grads are doing work for which only a high school degree is required.

SOME NEW THINKING REGARDING
SUCCESSFUL CHILDREN

Professor James Heckman is an economist at the University of Chicago. He is the Henry Schultz distinguished service professor of economics, professor of law at the Law School, director of the Center for the Economics of Human Development at the University, a senior research fellow at the American Bar Foundation, and a research associate at the National Bureau of Economic Research. Dr. Heckman shared the Nobel Memorial Prize in Economics in 2000 with Daniel McFadden for their pioneering work in econometrics and microeconomics. He is considered to be among the most influential economists in the world.

For years Dr. Heckman has studied, written about, and talked about the essential importance of noncognitive skills (socioemotional skills, later to be called character and grit) to success in life. He is a strong advocate of early intervention in the lives of underprivileged children who, if not raised in a loving, caring family, will have difficulties in both the cognitive and the noncognitive skills.

In 2012 Paul Tough produced a best-selling book titled: *How Children Succeed: Grit, Curiosity, and the Hidden Power of Character* that has influenced readers around the world. This book has been translated into twenty-five different languages. His writing brings professor Heckman's and other researchers work into the popular media and makes it great reading for millions of people concerned about how we're educating our children.

A twenty-minute video of his summary of this book is available on the website: www.elevateteachers.org. Look under resources—the essence of his work can be obtained in the first twelve minutes of the video. Paul Tough does a great job explaining his ideas. Viewing this video will dramatically improve understanding of what is coming next.

Following professor Heckman's work, author Tough separates the elements of success into two kinds of abilities. The first is the cognitive abilities. These skills have to do with the acquisition of knowledge, critical thinking skills, problem-solving abilities, and so on. These are the topics traditionally taught in the school systems.

The second set of skills he labels as character and grit—these are the noncognitive skills emphasized by professor Heckman. Author Tough points out that both sets of skills/values are important, in some instances the intellectual skills top the character and grit attributes, but in other cases, it is the other way around. Much of what is accomplished in the world is derived from character and grit.

Here are some examples to better define what is called character and grit.

Grit[5]

- Passion and perseverance for a long-term goal
- Having stamina
- Sticking with your future day in and day out—working very hard to make the future a reality
- Living life as a marathon

Character

- From dictionary—the mental and moral qualities distinctive to an individual
- A person's pattern of behavior, thoughts, and feelings that are based on sound principles, moral judgments, integrity, and the "line you never cross."
- It is evidenced by virtuous actions in both the moral and performance areas of one's life.
- Experts have divided character education generally into two parts— "performance character" (maximizing one's performance in every area of his or her life) and "moral character" (always choosing to do the right, honest, and ethical thing).

Character and grit can be described using seven high-level attributes:

1. Curiosity
2. Gratitude
3. Zest
4. Optimism
5. Self-control
6. Social intelligence
7. Grit

In the research building up to this book, several discussions with people working with poor people emphasized that poor children have grit; it takes grit to keep going day to day. This is true, but it is not the kind of grit being discussed. It is not grit aimed at a longer-term goal of obtaining a high school diploma, for example; it is more of a survival struggle.

The Success Equation

Here is an equation (figure 3.4) that combines school produced "book learning" with the more elusive noncognitive skills of character and grit. As has already been discussed, without hope this equation does not work.

What children need to be successful:

Figure 3.4.   Success equation.

Character and Grit Are Vital to Human Progress

Looking at how human endeavors are accomplished, too many times success is attributed to "brain power" when in fact, brainpower, all by itself, accomplishes very little. There are many brilliant people who accomplish well below their potential because they do not have the persistence to set and reach long-term goals. On the other hand, many can overcome shortfalls in intellect by simply "trying harder." There is a one-way substitution between intellect and grit.

TEXT BOX 3.2

Grit can substitute for intellect.
Intellect cannot be a substitute for grit.

For a young fourth grader, it is essential that they possess character and grit not just to produce success when they are thirty years old, but so they can be successful in class tomorrow, the day after, and so on. If they do not develop a longer-term vision for which to strive, they have no reason to perform on exams, do homework, and to actively participate in class. Teachers attribute a lack of character and grit for the unacceptable behavior of a proportion of each of their classes, the *disruptive* children.

Character and Grit Builds Self-Esteem

A by-product of a program that produces character and grit is self-esteem. Children with character and grit have their "act together" and can carry their heads high because they have the inner strength it requires to be in full control of themselves. They know how to deal with failure, and they have the pride of knowing that they "measure up" with anyone.

A good example, but later in life, is young people who join the U.S. Marines. They go into the military and are subjected to rigorous training that build within them a pride for the marines and their country that is vividly demonstrated when they visit home in their Marine uniforms. They have grown up; they have character and grit; they have self-esteem.

Repeating from chapter 2, many of the issues plaguing pre-K to 12 education today are due to a lack of character and grit by many of the students. Here are some specific problems:

1. Low teacher morale
2. Poor teacher retention

3. Poor student performance
4. The upcoming shortage in the production of teachers
5. Violence against teachers

Items 1–4 have already been covered. A very serious issue is item 5.

Violence against Teachers

According to a recent article published by the American Psychologist[6] (APA), 80 percent of teachers surveyed were victimized at school at least once in the current school year or prior year. Violence against teachers is a "national crisis," says Dr. Dorothy Espelage of the University of Illinois at Urbana-Champaign, who served as chair of the APA task force on Classroom Violence Directed at Teachers. And yet, the issue is generally ignored or at least underreported by the media and given inadequate attention by scholars—a deficiency that has widespread implications for school safety, the teaching profession, and student learning.

About half of the teachers who reported being victimized experienced harassment. Others reported property offenses, including theft and damage to property. And about one-quarter of these teachers experienced physical attacks. Harassment includes anything from obscene gestures, verbal threats, intimidation, and obscene remarks. With physical offenses, teachers widely reported objects being thrown at them and being physically attacked. The most severe and uncommon cases are physical attacks that result in a visit to a doctor.

Generally, educators and university professors believe that if there is a student behavioral problem, it is occurring because the teachers are not teaching in an engaging way. This logic is the primary reason that teachers take the blame for classroom management problems and low test results. Later chapters will show that there are some children in class that are unmanageable by the clear majority of the teachers.

Because no one directly associated with this book is involved with pre-K to 12 education, a school or teacher union, there are no political restraints on observations and research. The children are the manifestation of the problems. The reasons for their behavior will be revealed when the teachers do a root cause analysis to determine the real culprits. Much more on this topic will be presented in later chapters.

Is the Character/Grit Factor a Rediscovery?

In years past, when the social structure was significantly different, and highly family focused, the development of character and grit was unnoticed and taken for granted. Many children came from two-parent families where both of the parents focused on the family, assigned chores/tasks, and molded the children's character and grit. Boys often worked mowing yards, passing papers, doing farm work, assisting businesses, and so on. In addition, church attendance inculcated a set of values that were also supportive of growth in character and grit.

Today, the world has changed dramatically. The traditional family structure has changed in several ways:

1. Many families have two working adults.
2. Many poor children live with a single parent.
3. Sometimes the single parent lacks the skills to compete for a well-paying job—and must work multiple jobs to support the most meager lifestyle.
4. Many families are on welfare and are part of the multigenerational poor.
5. There is little farm work to assign to young people—farming is growing into a corporate business.
6. Children are engaged in after-class events to bolster resumes rather than teach employable skills.
7. Millions of low- and middle-income manufacturing jobs have been exported to low labor cost countries or replaced with automation—this hurts family income and spirit.
8. The influence of the church is waning as fewer and fewer people attend.
9. Our media culture molds thinking as to how a family should live, what they should eat and wear creating illusions that create discontent in some situations. A good example is foot ware—if it is not expensive, it isn't worth wearing.
10. There is a "I want it now" attitude in some young people—this is defeating the ability to patiently work to accomplish a difficult task.

These changes have inadvertently suppressed the role of character and grit in the lives of young people.

Failure Not Allowed

The U.S. culture is one where failure is not allowed. Always preserve the self-esteem of the children. Go to a youth baseball competition and watch how every child receives a trophy. There is a lot of reluctance to let children go home from the tourney empty-handed. So, what if they were not good enough to win or come in second, by golly they showed up and they tried and that's worthy of a trophy. These kids are very aware that their trophy has little value.

Once one investigates how to teach character and grit, it will be discovered that failure can be a great teacher, pick yourself up, dust yourself off, and try harder the next time. Children must learn how to deal with failure because they are going to face it no matter what they do. Learn the valuable lessons, and keep going.

School grades have been dramatically inflated in order to not cause the students to be saddened or angered by a bad grade. It doesn't matter much what the students do not know, that they didn't study hard only that they do not receive a low grade. A friend's daughter teaches courses at a university, and she's afraid to give students a grade below a C because they will raise so much hell.

The students have learned a new strategy to elevate their grade point average without regard to what they learned. Here the teacher is at fault for not giving the students proper feedback on their true abilities. She is "dumbing down" her courses and not motivating her students to excel.

A nephew's son graduated from a high school in Kentucky. The superintendent explained that the cords around the necks of many of the graduates exemplified that they were graduating with honors. In fact, 53 percent of the students were graduating with honors, and he was expecting the number to grow in the future. Isn't this just like the baseball tourney where everyone gets a trophy?

Think back into the past—who were the teachers most admired by most of the students? They were the ones who brought out the best in all the students, the ones who really taught material that was of great value. DePauw University hired a local certified public accountant, who had retired from his practice, to join the faculty. He was a great and loving professor, but he was famous for "pop" (unannounced) hour exams. Pop quizzes are one thing, but a pop hour exam is really tough.

His students kept up in his class and worked very hard. As time passed, they realized that he taught them real skills that added value to their success on the job. They loved him because he made them learn; he gave of himself to make them better people. Isn't this what all teachers are supposed to do?

Summarizing the Importance of Character and Grit

Paul Tough[7] and Angela Duckworth[8] have both written highly popular books about character and grit indicating a high degree of interest in these topics from the general public. Though there is need across all students for emphasis on character and grit, it is profoundly important for low-income students who suffer many disadvantages. Because of deficiencies in these two areas, many students do not have the interest or motivation to learn, and they become disruptive; their behavior is depriving other students, who are amenable to education, from significant quantities of classroom instructional time.

As will be seen later, the teachers believe that essentially all their students have the intellectual capability to pass the Indiana state assessment exams, but as will be seen, many do not because of deficiencies in character and grit.

The good news is that character and grit are teachable skills. In many homes, they are learned day to day from caring parents (or a caring parent) and the skills slowly develop over time by a kind comment here, a mild reprimand there, and sometimes stronger discipline all depending on the importance of the lesson and personality of the child. If not learned at home, there are four options:

1. Continue letting the students be disruptive and risking a school dropout later, or even criminal activity on the part of the student.
2. Expect the parents to do better and "shape up" their children.
3. Ask other organizations to help with this task.
4. Require the state and the school system to do the best they can at teaching the *disruptive*[9] students character and grit.

- Option 1. Will be the status quo unless changes in the schools are implemented; this will lead to continued mediocre performance.
- Option 2. The country has been waiting on this outcome for generations; it is unlikely to happen anytime soon.
- Option 3. Asking for help is always a good strategy assuming it is clear what they need to do. Elevate USA is an organization doing this in many schools.
- Option 4. This is the only viable option on the list. If change is not going to be coming from home, then the schools must step in and break the multiyear problems of school dropouts, students who graduate with no skills, some of whom turn to crime and end up in jail.

This research finds that there are ways to impact the shortcomings and to improve the noncognitive skills of most students. Later in the book some of these programs will be discussed. One thing is for sure that it will not be easy to accomplish what is needed for many students, but the old adage—pay me now or pay me later—is a reality.

Chapter 4

The Teachers Tell Their Story— A Research Study

INTRODUCTION TO RESEARCH STUDY

The content of this chapter is highly dependent upon the experience, thoughts, and knowledge of the teachers. It is important that the reader understands how many good ideas can come from the teachers, if only they are asked.

Maple Tree Elementary School (this is the fictitious name for a real school) is in Indianapolis, Indiana. This school provides free and reduced lunches to over 80 percent of its children as it is a high-poverty school. In the fall of 2012, the state of Indiana issued its first official school grades to over 2,100 public and nonpublic schools. Maple Tree's first grade was a "D." This was painful for the staff but it was completely in line with the sequence of "practice" grades given for several years.

The teachers were perplexed because the state's assignment of school grades were assigned with test results as the only consideration. The teachers believe that one additional factor should be considered as the grades are assigned; some adjustment must be made for the low socioeconomic status of the children in poor schools.

In October of 2012, a phone call to Son John made this proposal: "Your teaching story needs to be told. The public needs to understand what is going on in your school." In consultation with the other three teachers, there was some concern with becoming "cross ways" with school management so the decision was that it was too risky.

No further thought was given to the proposed project until March of 2013. By this point in time, the teachers were so frustrated they told John to set up a meeting. They needed help; they needed someone who cared about their plight. Meetings began in one of the classrooms. One thing was apparent at the outset—their attitudes and emotions were identical to John's. This was a relief since there was the potential that his frustrations were not shared by the other teachers showing that there was personal bias in John's emotions. They were all of one mind; they needed help! It was agreed early on that the teachers would not comment on anyone in a leadership position in their district; this topic was "off limits."

Applying Business Problem Solving to Education

As a seasoned facilitator, having facilitated approximately sixty central Indiana nonprofit organizations through long-range plans, working with the teachers was new ground. It was decided that the process to be used would be the application of what industry calls the Total Quality Program[1]; at the beginning, there was some floundering but things soon fell into place, and the group was off and running.

BRIEF HISTORY OF TOTAL QUALITY PROGRAM— THE PROCESS USED IN STUDY

In the late 1970s and 1980s, the United States was losing the manufacturing battle to Japan, primarily because the Japanese had superior quality. This was particularly true with automobiles. A Japanese car could be purchased without the seemingly inevitable two or three return trips to the dealer to finally get everything working properly. U.S. industry finally awakened to the role that quality played in the buying decision for many items. In the process, there was demonstrable evidence that high quality paid for itself.

The Four Steps

Below are the four steps used by many companies. They were used in this research to identify and improve education at Maple Tree Elementary:

1. If you want to understand and improve a job, ask the people who do the job.
2. Speak with data.
3. Look for root cause.
4. Steal ideas without shame.

Using the Process with the Teaches

Step 1: Ask the Teachers How to Improve their Jobs
    As the team began to meet as a working group, it was quite clear that the teachers relished the opportunity to describe their job and its associated

frustrations. It was apparent with this group that though the higher administration often speaks for the teachers, it seldom speaks to them. Once this stage began, the emotions were clearly deep and troubled. The teachers were not upset about teaching; they were upset because of their inability to teach. Too many interruptions, too many extra "bureaucratic satisfying" assignments, too many unruly children.

TEXT BOX 4.1

The teachers were not upset about teaching; they were upset because of their inability to teach.

Detailed discussions would involve the teachers offering their perspective on the current topic; these thoughts would be recorded and e-mailed back to the teachers. They would make changes then the various inputs harmonized into an effective summary of the meeting.

TEXT BOX 4.2

It was apparent with this group that though the higher administration often speaks for the teachers, it seldom speaks to them.

Step 2: Speak with Data

Step 2 is very important for the quantification of teachers' frustrations. The teachers selected three metrics to be measured. The three measures are:

1. Multiple requests to follow directions
2. Failure to actively listen
3. Bad attitude/conflict

These are all disruptions for each class in varying magnitudes. An admonition to a particular student to listen better will most likely not be a major event, but it does take away from teaching time. A severe disruption resulting from a student's profane and violent outburst could affect the class for many minutes, perhaps many hours. All of these add up to lost instructional time and a poor learning environment. General admonitions to the entire class were not recorded; they had to be associated with a particular student; this is the only way to quantify the impact of each student's behavior.

Step 3: Look for Root Cause

Step 3 will be used to attempt to get to the bottom of the behavioral issues for *disruptive* children (will be defined below). On several occasions, the "why" question is asked. The journey to the root cause ends for this study once the "why" questions are exhausted.

Step 4: Steal Ideas without Shame

Step 4 will be used in the second phase of this research. The task is to look for successful ideas wherever they can be found. Chapter 5 will document five different schools and how they approach teaching and molding children in need. These example programs offer a number of "good ideas that can be put to work in many schools."

LETTING THE TEACHERS TALK ABOUT THEIR JOBS

The first step is to ask the teachers how to improve their job. In the first team meeting, the teachers took out a fresh piece of paper and answered two questions about the D grade their school recently received. These questions were:

1. What are the factors that caused your school to be graded D?
2. What must change to elevate this grade?

These are the teachers' answers; they have been harmonized to reduce the number of lines of text. Once the list was passed back to them, they agreed on this set of responses. As will be seen later in the book, many of their concerns are in accord with not only independent research but also with supporting data and documentation. This is a good picture of what and how they are thinking.

Here are their answers to these two questions:

1. What are the factors that caused your school to be graded D?

   - There are no real consequences for failing tests, misbehavior, or most anything else.
   - Children have a sense of entitlement; they want things given to them without having to work for them.

- Parents do not care about how/what their kids do in school.
- Kids do not care about learning or passing exams.
- Home life is a major detriment to academic performance; for example, some are not well fed, some stay up late, and some parents are not literate themselves.
- Parental expectations for kids are low—some of their cultures do not value education.
- They come to school unprepared educationally, emotionally, and socially. Socially they do not know how to handle conflict—their natural and immediate response is to reply to conflict with conflict.
- Teachers cannot positively influence their lives outside of school.

2. What must change to elevate this grade?

- The number of serious behavioral problems in each classroom must be dramatically reduced.
- Students with serious discipline problems must be subject to harsh punishment if necessary.
- Children are variables, not widgets. ELL students and Special Ed students will not grow at a "typical" rate.
- The severest offenders must be removed from the classrooms and sent to alternative schools where they do not interrupt the learning of the children who want to learn.
- Parents must be held accountable.
- There must be consequences.

The teachers were very frustrated because of the lack of discipline in their school and township. Sending a child to the principal's office turns out to be a waste of time for both the teacher and the child. Nothing happens in the principal's office. What the teachers began doing, it's a terrible alternative, is to place the offending child in the room of another fourth-grade teacher. Usually the receiving teacher then sits the child down and ignores him or her since he or she is not in the flow of the current lesson.

The other theme is the lack of consequences—there are no consequences for much of anything. Occasionally a student will be suspended for a few days, but that only proves to be a hardship for the working parent(s).

The teachers' frustration and sense of helplessness were difficult to watch. They were all well trained and experienced, but they were feeling bad about how little impact they were having on the lives of their children. As will be seen later, most of the children were well mannered and wanted to learn but a group of students made it very, very difficult for the rest of the class to learn and for the teachers to teach.

THE KIDS ARE SMART ENOUGH

The third step in the process is to look for root cause. Here the goal is to dig deep into the activities and environment of the teachers to find the "bottom of the whys" that explain why things are the way they are.

An Important Question

Before the team could move on with this project, the teachers were asked a tough question. "Are your children intellectually capable of passing the state assessment exam?" If the answer is yes, we move on, if no, the research project stops in its tracks. The teachers say:

TEXT BOX 4.3

In our judgment, our students, with some exceptions, have the native intellectual capacity to pass the ISTEP exam or do well on any assessment test. At the current time, there are barriers that get in the way of their ability to grow and apply these skills in an effective way.

The four teachers' answers were unequivocal, "In our judgment, our students, with some exceptions, have the native intellectual capacity to pass the ISTEP exam or do well on any assessment test. At the current time, there are barriers that get in the way of their ability to grow and to apply these skills in an effective way." The teachers' declaration that the students have the intellectual capability to pass the ISTEP exams certainly applies to the *disruptive* students as well—they are classified as *disruptives* because of behavior, not because they are intellectually limited.

TEXT BOX 4.4

This book will emphasize several times that it is the behavior of a group of children that is at issue, not their mental capacity.

The equivocation, "with some exceptions" expressed above, means that this population is no different from any other. There is a normal curve of intellectual skills and some students will always fall on the lower tail. The issue of barriers will be discussed later. Also, the teachers were very sympathetic with special ed children or children with deficient language skills. Their special situations alone will not land them in a *disruptive* group.

Is there any proof that the teachers are correct in their assessment of the children's innate abilities? One great way to prove their capabilities would be to give them a test, and they all pass. This has been done, and the resulting outcome led to the school being graded a D. Looking at other poor children in Indiana and their performance on the ISTEP exam may provide insight as to whether the teachers contention is accurate, that is, to see if many of them can do well on the exam.

Is the Grade That a School Receives Tied to Their Student's Socioeconomic Level? (Traditional Public Schools Only)

The following analysis is a bit complicated and may not be something that all readers want to tackle. Here are two paths to follow: a short one that immediately gives the answer and a long one that leads to the path through the analysis. This approach is presented because the conclusion of this section is extremely important to understand how poverty does not affect student accomplishment.

The Short Path

The conclusion is that there is only a *very weak* association between a school's socioeconomic status and the performance of the students on standardized assessment exams. More quantitatively, if high-poverty schools are defined to be schools in the 70 to 100 percent range of free and reduced lunch percentages, only 29 percent of the schools are graded D or F.

This again reinforces the point that poor children can excel if the proper conditions are established. This supports the teacher's contention that the children have the intellectual capability to pass the assessment exams but it refutes their contention that socioeconomic levels should be in the grading equation. Now, skip down to: *Should the School's Grade Consider its Level of Poverty?* (page 48).

The Longer Path

A database was created that places, alongside the school's letter grade, the average percentage of free and reduced meals for that school. The percentage of students on free and reduced lunches, though not perfect, is a proxy for the level of poverty in a school.

Sorting this database produces table 4.1 for all Indiana public schools. This presentation appears shows that there is a relationship between a school's letter grade and their average meal percent. No fancy correlation analysis is needed here, as common sense works just fine. In other words, notice that as the school grades go down, the meal percent goes up. The obvious conclusion is that the poor children drag the school grade down. This, at this level of detail, supports the teacher's argument that some consideration should be given to high-poverty schools in the assignment of school grades.

Look at a Possible School Grade Scheme

If the above relationship is very strong, all the State Department of Education needs is a grading scale that might look like the one in table 4.2. With this table, they simply assign the grades based on the free and reduced lunch percent (this table is entirely fictional and is presented to prove a point).

For example, a school meal percent of 84 percent would result in a D grade. This implies that the level of poverty in their school already determines a student's intellectual performance. This violates the teacher's declaration about intellectual capability and it would also be terribly disappointing to find that there is such a strong link between poverty and student performance.

Table 4.3 shows the range of free and reduced meal percentages for any given school grade.

Table 4.1. Indiana School Grades Decline as Meal Percentage Increases 2013–2014

School Grade	Free and Reduced Meal Percent for School
A	44.4
B	51.6
C	58.4
D	71.8
F	82.55

Table 4.2. Possible School-Grading Scheme

Free and Reduced Lunch Percent	Official School Grade
0–48	A
49–54	B
55–65	C
66–84	D
85+	F

Dig deeper—table 4.3 gives the range of the meal percentages for each school's letter grade. The range is a statistical term that defines the smallest and largest values for a variable. The A graded school data ranged from a very low meal percentage of 1.1 all the way to one school that was 98.3 percent (a very high-poverty school). This is very exciting as A grades are expected in low-poverty neighborhoods but not in neighborhoods where 98.3 percent of the students receive free and reduced lunches. This is the first hint of really good news. As will soon be demonstrated, there are many A graded schools with meal percentages in the seventy-plus range.

Focus attention on schools in the 70–100 percent range of meal percentages—this is the working definition of "high poverty" used in this book. Table 4.4 shows that there are more A, B, and C graded schools in each of the ranges up to 100 percent than D and F graded schools. In total, for the meal percent range of 70–100 percent, there are 273 A, B, and C graded schools and 109 D and F graded schools.

This data clearly illustrates that the meal percentages have a small impact on the school grade. If someone says a school is in the 70–100 percent range of free and reduced meal percentages, there is only a 29 percent chance that it is a D or F graded school. This is a very significant conclusion.

Table 4.4 gives the data showing that there are more A, B, and C graded schools than D and F graded schools in the high-poverty schools.

Table 4.3. Indiana School Grades Range Up and Down the Meal Percentages 2013–2014

School Grade	Lower-Limit Meal Percent	Upper-Limit Meal Percent
A	1.1	98.3
B	7.1	95.5
C	16.4	94.2
D	33.2	100
F	53.5	97.6

Table 4.4. Poor Children Can and Do Succeed! School Year 2013–2014

Meal % Interval	No. Schools with A, B, or C Grade	No. Schools with D or F Grade	Percentage A, B, or C Grade
70–79.9	134	38	78
80–89.9	98	49	67
90+	41	22	65
	273	109	71

Should the School's Grade Consider Its Level of Poverty?

The four teachers on the study team made the declaration about sufficient students' intellectual capability quoted earlier. At the same time, they argue that any school-grading scheme must consider the socioeconomic level of the children's families. Are these two points in conflict? The analysis just presented shows that the high-poverty children have the intellectual ability so why should socioeconomic level matter? This section establishes that socioeconomic level should not be considered in the grading scheme.

TEXT BOX 4.5

If someone tells you a school is in the 70–100 percent free and reduced meal percentages, there is only a 29 percent chance that it is a D or F graded school.

This is a very significant conclusion.

These results strongly support the teacher's contention that the students have the intellectual capability to do well on the state's assessment exam. Of course, it does not prove that *their* fourth-grade students can pass the ISTEP exam, but it does show that many low-socioeconomic students around the state are doing well on the test.

Looking further, these results support what Cynthia J. Johnson says in the journal *The Association for Middle Level Education.*[2]

> There is a misperception that low-socioeconomic level produces low outcomes. This is far from the truth and such beliefs can stifle what children can accomplish or be allowed to accomplish. Multigenerational poverty stricken children have hopes just like other children. Children who live in poverty can meet high expectations and standards. Once we in the world of education understand and embrace this truth, outcomes for children in poverty will change.

Indiana Hit Parade of Schools[3]

There are 114 Indiana schools in the high-poverty range that are A graded schools. These are schools that merit special recognition for their ability to reach low-level socioeconomic children though little attention is directed to these schools. It is one thing to earn an A grade in high-income cities like Zionsville or Carmel, but quite another to earn that grade in a high-poverty school. Table 4.5 gives the ten A graded schools that had the highest

Table 4.5. Indiana Hit Parade of Schools 2013–2014

	School District	School Name	County	Grade	Meal %
105	Muncie Community Schools	Longfellow Elementary School	Delaware	A	93.5
106	Gary Community School Corp	Daniel Hale Williams Elem Sch	Lake	A	93.7
107	School City of East Chicago	George Washington Elem School	Lake	A	94.2
108	School City of East Chicago	William McKinley Elementary Sch	Lake	A	94.2
109	M S D Wayne Township	Stout Field Elementary School	Marion	A	94.4
110	Anderson Community School Corp	Anderson Elementary School	Madison	A	96.4
111	School City of Hammond	Lafayette Elementary School	Lake	A	96.8
112	School City of East Chicago	Abraham Lincoln Elementary Sch	Lake	A	97.7
113	Evansville Vanderburgh Sch Corp	Delaware Elementary School	Vanderburgh	A	97.9
114	School City of East Chicago	Carrie Gosch Elementary School	Lake	A	98.3

percentages of students on free and reduced lunches (Meal %); these are the most economically challenged schools. Appendix A gives the entire list of 114 schools.

BONUS RESULTS—CHARTER SCHOOLS DO NOT MEASURE UP

To deduce the results shown in the prior chapter, a large EXCEL database needed to be assembled. This database can reveal other interesting things about schools in Indiana.

All the important school results for this book are derived from two school years 2012–2013 and 2013–2014. These years are comparable because the tests were of similar difficulty and the school-grading schemes the same. In 2014–2015, the test was oriented toward college preparation and it was so long and difficult that the results were not used. The very latest results would be the school year 2015–2016, but this was another difficult year.

How the Three Different Types of Schools
Compare to Each Other?

To create these results, the 2,095 Indiana schools were divided into three different school types (each school type includes elementary, middle, and high schools):

1. Traditional public schools
2. Religious/private/other schools
3. Charter schools

Once the division was made, a simple logic equation converted the letter grades to a numerical value. The scheme is: A=4, B=3, C=2, D=1, and F=0. Once the numerical values were assigned, the results were added up and divided by the number of schools of that school type to obtain the average. This is identical to the way a university determines the average grade point for a group of students, for example, all freshmen. Table 4.6 shows those averages for the three school types.

Look at the third column (Avg. GPA 2014), the religious/independent schools have an average school grade of a 3.4, say a B+. This is the standard by which the other two school types will be assessed. The traditional public schools have a 3.1, a B; that's fairly close, 0.3, to the religious/independent schools allowing the conclusion that the traditional public schools in Indiana are doing very well, at least for these two years.

The charter schools average a 1.6, a D+ or C–. This was a big surprise to find that the charter schools scored so low. In the press, they are touted as the hope for educational reform since they have the freedom to experiment with different teaching styles and curriculum.

Recently the year 2016 different school type grades were computed and added to the table (see column 4). Comparing the most recent test scores with the 2014 numbers shows that the most recent test was much more difficult since all schools, but charter schools, went down by a significant amount. The gap between the traditional public schools and the religious/private schools has grown to 0.3 (3.0–2.6) illustrating that the religious/private schools did

Table 4.6.   Calculation of Grade Point Average by School Type

School Type	Avg. GPA 2013	Avg. GPA 2014	New Data! Avg. GPA 2016	Number of Schools
Traditional public	2.9	3.1	2.6	1,758
Religious/independent	3.2	3.4	3.0	279
Charter schools	1.5	1.6	1.7	58

considerably better than the public schools on the more difficult exam. This illustrates that when the "going gets tough," the nonpublic schools do better.

A pleasant surprise is the performance of the charter schools. The other two school types grades went down with the more difficult exam, but the charters went up! This is great, though they are still well behind the other two types.

Keep in mind that the 2014–2015 ISTEP exam was so difficult it was essentially "tossed out" and not used.

Googling "problems with charter schools" will yield a surprising number of hits; there is a general feeling in the country that many more schools should be charter schools. Their results do not support that contention at all!

Valerie Strauss of the *Washington Post*[4] wrote an article in May of 2014 titled, *A Dozen Problems with Charter Schools*. She points out that there is a great deal of evidence that there are many big problems in the charter sector. A recent report from Pennsylvania shows that only one in six of their charter schools is performing at a high level[5]. This report was released by Representative James Roebuck, chairman of the Pennsylvania House Education Committee. All together, there are 28 top-performing schools out of 162 total charters. These twenty-eight schools are not using traditional methods but offer innovative programs.

Here are some of the problem issues with charter schools:

1. Most of the schools are not really helping students improve their academic performance—this is illustrated by the just presented charter school grades of 1.6 or 1.7.
2. Some charter schools are hurting children. Because of tight budgets, many schools offer a very narrow curriculum.
3. Hedge fund managers invest in charter school corporations because they see them as "cash cows."
4. The industry is rife with fraud and corruption.
5. Though charters are public schools, they are not always transparent in their dealings.
6. Charters do not take students who will be too expensive to manage—they "skim."
7. They are a force to resegregate our schools.
8. Charters drain needed resources from needy public schools.
9. They do not innovate as was originally envisioned in their creation.
10. It is hard to shut down bad charter schools.

A Bad Charter School Experience

Two grandchildren attended a charter high school in Indianapolis. Their school had a difficult time hiring and keeping faculty. The granddaughter left

Table 4.7.   Where Are the Bad Grades? Year 2013–2014

School District	Total Schools	D and F Grades	Percentage D & F
Charter schools	58	34	59
Indianapolis Public Schools	65	32	49
South Bend Community Sch. Corp.	34	15	44
Gary Community Sch. Corp.	16	10	63
Evansville Vanderburgh Sch. Corp.	35	9	26
School City of Hammond	20	6	30
MSD Warren Twp.	17	6	35
Ft. Wayne Comm. Sch.	49	5	10
Comm. Sch. of Frankfort	5	4	80
Total		121	
Total D and F grades in Indiana		217	

and spent her junior and senior years at Lawrence North High School, Indianapolis, and enjoyed the experience. The grandson started his senior year at the charter school but only had two teachers for five classes. They did hire a math teacher, but he left after two weeks. The grandson also transferred to Lawrence North High School.

The next logical question to ask is where are the low grades concentrated. Table 4.7 shows the nine school districts that produce 56 percent of the state's D and F grades.

The table shows that the charter schools (not really a school district) are the largest producers of D and F grades in Indiana. As would be expected, the larger metropolitan areas are producing most of the low school grades. Because the press targets metropolitan schools for many of their negative stories, this relatively small number of schools spoils the reputation of most of the public schools.

HOW CLASSROOM TIME IS WASTED

Recently, while riding in the car with the radio tuned to the local public radio station, there was a discussion about a young man who had been suspended from school, not expelled but suspended. The hostess was interviewing a social worker whose job was to prepare the young man to return to school. The discussion took place under a dark cloud, a cloud of supposed school/teacher failure, for allowing this suspension to happen. The tone of the conversation was subdued, and great effort was expended to blame everyone but the young man. As this story unfolded, it was apparent that the social worker did not fully comprehend that a class is made up of three different student types. Any student whose behavior leads to a school suspension is probably what the teachers in this study call a *disruptive* student. This student label will be explained in the section beginning on page 56.

The Anatomy of a Suspension

To better understand how this suspension looks from a teacher's point of view, a deeper study will be made of a typical suspension case. This discussion is positioned around a student who is ultimately suspended to place focus on a bad situation. Not only will this case study be helpful to explain the behavior of a *disruptive* student, it will illustrate how lost instruction time is created as the teacher deals with the various events. It also illustrates a series of negative deposits into the teacher's emotional bank account, a topic to be addressed shortly.

Figure 4.1 (The Anatomy of a Suspension) is a fabricated time line showing that the offending student has had a series of issues in the classroom over the days before the suspension. This is not an actual case, but it is a series of plausible disruptions that would be likely with a *disruptive* student.

What do the times mean? Here is a summary of lost time for each of the pictured days—there were many more days like these, but five is enough to make this point. The times refer to the amount of time the entire class was disrupted out of their "learning environment."

1. Day 4:   28 minutes
2. Day 3:   23 minutes
3. Day 2:   0 minutes (student was absent from school)
4. Day 1:   21 minutes
5. Day 0:   39 minutes
Total lost time: 111 minutes
Average: 28 minutes for the days the student was in school

What Is a Learning Environment?

A learning environment is an environment where positive learning is taking place. It doesn't necessarily mean a room where every student is paying rapt attention to the teacher—it could be a group activity with a lot of commotion but the activity is focused enough for a project to be completed, which leads to learning. As will be read later, the time wasted by a classroom disruption can go well beyond the length of the disruption.

Depending on the severity of the disruption, it might take two to three times the actual disruption time for the students to "get back into learning mode." The teachers will estimate this time for each of the three measured lost time disruptions later.

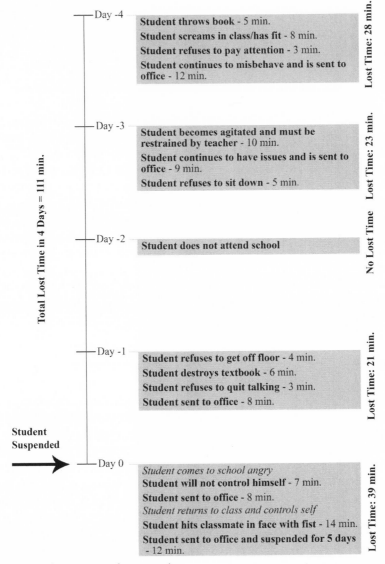

Figure 4.1.   The anatomy of a suspension.

The Eye Opener

The Anatomy of a Suspension described the time-consuming activities of only one of the teacher's *disruptive* students.

TEXT BOX 4.6

A typical classroom in the school studied will have an average of five to six *disruptive* students!

Just imagine what it's like for the teacher to try to teach and manage five to six children who are essentially uncontrollable. Should the teachers be criticized for their inability to manage their classroom? Theoretically yes, but practically it depends. It depends upon the skill of the teachers, school, and classroom rules, and how well the administration supports the teachers, involvement of parents, and other factors. Of course, the big factor is the behavior of their students.

School administrators say, "There are teachers who can manage these classrooms." The response, "By all means, bring them in because you need them in a hurry." The point is that there are some teachers that can manage *disruptive* children but they are few and far between. Most schools of education do not teach the kind of skills needed to manage *disruptive* students.

THE TEACHER'S EMOTIONAL BANK ACCOUNT

Teachers, especially in low-income schools, carry heavy burdens. They are expected to do more and more while their actual teaching time is being reduced by practice exams, other types of assessment exams beyond the important state exams, by the mentally challenged and by disruptive students.

More and more paper work is demanded by bureaucrats from both the state and federal levels. In low-income areas, obtaining support from some parents, of *disruptive* students for example, is very hard to do, and the four teachers often are negatively affected by their infrequent interactions with parents, assuming they can even find someone to talk with. This all leads to the idea of a teacher's emotional bank account. Figure 4.2 is a picture to make the point.

Generally, in most of today's public schools, teachers are working with a negative emotional bank account balance. Public school teacher morale is low throughout much of the nation; enrollment in schools of education is dropping, teacher status is low. Later, in chapter 5, discussion will highlight an outstanding private school in Indianapolis called The Oaks Academy, they position their teachers high in the Positive Account Balance, because they are receiving great satisfaction from changing children's lives.

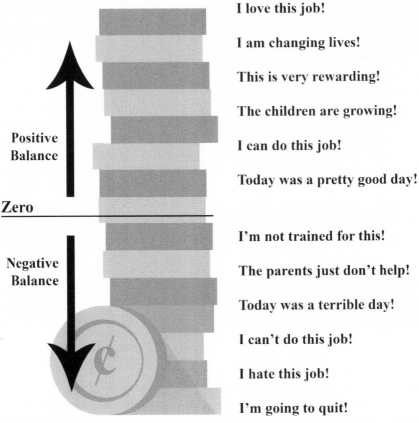

Figure 4.2.   Teacher's emotional bank account.

In talking with teachers about this concept, it is amazing how little it takes to make a positive deposit. It could be a complementary call from a parent, students saying how much they enjoy class, and/or a note from a parent or child. The general lack of positive feedback makes most anything good have a big impact. On the other side of the ledger, they absorb many significant withdrawals with amazing aplomb.

THE SPECTRUM OF STUDENTS

The teachers say that the makeup of their classes (they add, any class) can be described by placing each student on a spectrum of student types. As would be expected, there are good students and bad; there are students who listen to instructions and do their work; and there are others who are not so good. As this discussion unfolded, this spectrum was established:

The Engaged Student . . . . The Followers . . . . The Disruptive Student

The teachers are very concerned about a proportion of their students (the *disruptives*) who are so difficult to manage; those students who dramatically affect the learning process of the entire classroom. This proportion, for this school at this point in time, will be estimated below.

While students seldom clearly fall into a clear type, and can vary over time, there are three types that are going to be defined to oversimplify for the sake of discussion.

Below are the teacher's definitions of these three student states.

THE ENGAGED STUDENT

Engaged students can be counted on to act with integrity the majority of the time. They are the ones who stay in their seats and keep working quietly if the teacher steps out of the room. When their teacher is teaching, their eyes are either on the teacher, or on the material that is being taught. Either way, they are actively listening and participating in the lesson. When given an assignment, they get busy immediately. They sit at their desk or in their assigned spot and work. They raise their hand if they have trouble.

They never call out if they have a question. It is very rare that *engaged* students do not get their work done, as these students are self-motivated learners. *Engaged* students, in the rare instance that they don't follow procedures, will accept consequences without attitude and are always honest with the teacher. *Engaged* students are often the most academically successful students. Should these students ever need a call home (which is usually unnecessary), the parents are supportive, and the problem stops.

THE FOLLOWERS

Follower students are the most complex and are often the most common type of students. This category of students is a "follower" and is heavily influenced by the students around them. If a *follower* student is around a group of *engaged* students, then he or she will behave like an *engaged* student. More often however, when a *follower* student is around a number of *disruptive* students, then he or she will behave like the *disruptive* student. Academically, *follower* students vary across the intellectual spectrum and follow a typical student talent distribution curve.

Most *follower* students get their homework and class work completed. However, if a *follower* student is working with a *disruptive* student, the assignment tends not to get completed. *Follower* students are generally more willing to accept the consequences of their choices, but some *follower* students deny that they did anything or give attitude. A phone call home generally receive a positive response from a parent. However, the behavior is less likely to be resolved. It may stop for a few days, but it eventually comes back.

THE DISRUPTIVE STUDENTS

Disruptive students are the ones who rarely make good choices in the classroom. They cannot be trusted to make good decisions when left alone. They rarely do their homework and getting them to complete class work is very difficult, often requiring the teacher to stand in close proximity to them. These students rarely take responsibility for their actions and blame others for their choices. When corrected, these students can become belligerent, attitudinal, or act as if they don't care.

These students are frequently bullies and do not hesitate to initiate conflict against their peers and sometimes against their teachers. Many are also highly subversive, not out-and-out causing conflict, but often creating conflict by spreading rumors or instigating others to fight. A phone call home does not solve the problem. These parents have gotten phone calls from their child's teachers for years about the same problems.

The sad reality is that many parents of these students have as many issues as the student and can become confrontational with the teacher. Some tell the teacher to never call again, others become verbally abusive, and a few need to be escorted from the building. The other response is "nothing." Phone calls are not returned nor will the parent come to the school to conference with the teacher, unless required by the office to do so. For a *disruptive* student, many of their problems can be traced directly to their challenging home environment.

Important Note: This book deals with children in poor families and what can be done to improve their academic progress. As reviewers of this research advise, *disruptive* students are also present in many high-end schools. They exhibit some of the behavior, especially disrespect for the teachers and fellow students, described above and can be a major problem for the teachers to manage.

The following is a deeper look at some of the social realities of *disruptive* children. Some live a very uncertain life outside of the classroom with many family issues that many cannot even imagine. For some of them, going home is not a good thing. The teachers say, "We teach children who have been abused, who are or have been homeless, and who have little or no parental support." Many times, there is no father in the picture and mom is on welfare or working two, maybe three, jobs just to keep a roof over her family. As a result, here are some of the student behaviors experienced:

1. They have a pronounced "I don't care" attitude, usually because they feel the people and institutions around them don't care about them.
2. They do not respect others and certainly not their teachers.
3. They are very difficult to manage in a classroom situation.
4. Their parents often are not involved in many/any aspects of their educational growth.
5. They do not exhibit an understanding of the value of an education.
6. If parents are contacted about a student issue and they agree to work with the student, it is often unusual for them to take any action. Because of these issues, test scores suffer for the entire classroom/school.

Teachers try to reach each and every child. Teachers eat with them, talk one-on-one with them, work with them, and let them know that they genuinely care about them. The teachers see these kids for who they are and try to understand the issues they deal with day in and day out. Teachers know which students have parents going through divorce, which students have a parent in jail or on welfare, or which students have been beaten or abused.

Children are in school about 7 hours each day with only 3.7 hours in ISTEP-based instruction time with their teacher in their rooms (yes, the teachers teach to the test). Considering an entire calendar year (365 days), the children are under the direct influence of their teachers and school about 14 percent of their time. With so many problem students, it is very hard for teachers to deal with the difficult and complicated issues that some of their students face.

NUMBER OF STUDENTS BY DEFINITION

Once the definitions were finalized, each teacher was asked to estimate what percentage of his or her class were there in each category. The display below gives the average for all four classes of each student type.

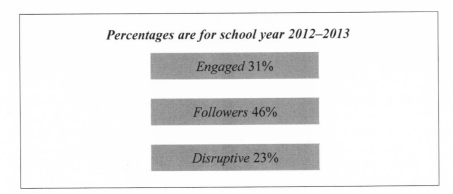

Percentages are for school year 2012–2013

Engaged 31%

Followers 46%

Disruptive 23%

Looking at these numbers one begins to develop a better understanding of what a classroom is like for this D-graded school. With a class size of twenty-four to twenty-five, these numbers show there will be from five to six *disruptive* students in every class. The *follower* students are more highly influenced by the *disruptives* than they are by the *engaged*. Consequently, a large number of the *followers* will, on occasion, fall into the *disruptive* category.

This means that at times, the classroom could be composed of a majority of *disruptives*. These situations lead to classroom chaos and severely test the teacher's patience and endurance plus result in sizeable reductions in classroom instruction time.

TEXT BOX 4.8

It is terribly wrong for this group of disruptive students to deprive the balance of the class, students who are amenable to education, from an opportunity to learn and excel.

Picture yourself as a teacher in one of these classrooms. Teaching has appeal as a profession because of how much influence a teacher can have in a child's life. Early on, the profession sounds wonderful with a perfect mix of service and teaching. Soon it is discovered that far too little time is spent in teaching. Often, there is the feeling that the classroom is in a constant state of upheaval because it is so difficult to control the some of the students. This is a terrible morale-killer; there must be a way out of this school.

Which schools will support teaching and have good discipline? Are there schools where the teachers have a say in how things are done? Which schools engage parents to make the school better? Will it ever happen at this school? This may be the time to give up teaching and look for a better skill-fit. The

National Education Association reports that 33 percent of new teachers leave the profession in three years; 46 percent leave in five years.

Was 2012–2013 an Unusual Year?

The 2013–2014 (note this is the next year) fourth-grade teachers were asked to review the definitions of the different types of students and to break out the percentages of three kinds of students. The two years are almost identical in the percentages of the different types. So, the school year that was used in the paper was typical at this point in time illustrating that these teachers face these situations for multiple years.

Examples of Disruptive Student Behaviors

There will always be the lingering question, "Is it the students or is it the teacher?" Look at some examples of *disruptive* students' behavior from the press, studies, and so on and make up your own mind if a teacher should be expected to control this kind of behavior. *Keep in mind that these examples are not from the target school.* Many of these stories are about older children—well beyond the fourth grade. As the children grow older, the events grow far more serious.

1. "He was mad at me because I made him redo a math test so he walked over to the classroom door. When I told him I would need to call the office if he left the room without permission he proceeded to slam his own leg in the door about five times, then he looked at me and said, 'Now my leg hurts and I'm going to tell everyone it was your fault.'"[6]
2. "He was 5 and in kindergarten. I watched him at recess walk over to another boy and punch him in the face. With no emotion on his face. No feelings. When I found out who the kid was, turns out his grandfather went to prison for murdering a lot of prostitutes."[7]
3. "Then, all of a sudden, (and this sounds like it was pre-planned and done with military-style execution), this lone kid got up and stood on the table and started singing 'It's Oh so Quiet' by Björk. The teacher stood there in bemusement and confusion wondering what the hell was going on, until the bit where they sang the line 'and so peaceful until.' Next thing, the whole class just went berserk and absolutely ransacked the classroom, forcing the teacher to flee, and the lesson got abandoned. I heard the classroom literally got destroyed as the kids went on the rampage."[8]

    a. *Note that points 5, 6, 7, 8, and 9 all come from the endnote*[9]

4. "Scores of teachers in Western Pennsylvania are the targets of assaults by students each year, according to state data."

5. "We need to recognize teaching is a hazardous occupation," said Dorothy Espelage, a professor of counseling and educational psychology at the University of Illinois Champaign.

6. "In February 2012, she saw a student throw another boy against a locker and begin beating him on the floor. She crouched down behind the 14-year-old and told him to stop. 'I knew the kid. I had him in class, and I knew when he gets emotionally upset, he gets physical,' said Swigart, who was a seventh-grade math teacher. 'He reached up and grabbed me by the neck and flipped me over his shoulder, and I wound up on the floor between them.' Swigart, who was 51 at the time, suffered a concussion and a shoulder injury. She was out of school about four weeks while she recovered."

7. A Philadelphia high school teacher was hospitalized in December when two students beat him in a dispute over a cellphone.

8. An experienced kindergarten teacher from Racine, Wisconsin, reviewed the original paper and said the description of student behavior was appropriate for her kindergarten children. She once had a student who bashed a fellow student's head against a urinal and the child needed stitches.[10]

9. "A Memphis Tennessee teacher relates this story. Once student behavior reached a new low in a local middle school she quit her job. She was verbally abused by the students, called gay, lesbian, a dyke and even white girl. Students said this to her: Who the f-bomb do you think you're talking to? And shut the F..k up. No punishment was given to any student for this behavior."[11]

10. List of violent classroom episodes from YouTube videos.

https://www.youtube.com/watch?v=hllCSqHPI_g
https://www.youtube.com/watch?v=7AQWYAeU7G4
https://www.youtube.com/watch?v=xDifkMzSLuw
https://www.youtube.com/watch?v=g7BR09BtgcA
https://www.youtube.com/watch?v=CLmQ1KdhRO0
https://www.youtube.com/watch?v=-1eUADIdHWU
https://www.youtube.com/watch?v=Gg_44_cIjEM
https://www.youtube.com/watch?v=oFLMJJ58xyg
https://www.youtube.com/watch?v=-1eUADIdHWU

MEASURING LOST TIME

When the teachers describe a typical day with all their interruptions two things are apparent:

1. Considerable classroom instructional time is wasted dealing with repeated instructions, getting the students attention and conduct.

2. The "learning environment" in the classroom is not good, particularly when the *disruptive* students can be so impactful.

The second step of the process is to gather data—as is said in industry, "speak with data." Data is objective and will eliminate a lot of the possible confusion in the describing the magnitude of the problem to others. To this end, the school's teachers set up a measurement system to quantify the "lost instructional time."

Metrics—Gathering Data

To illustrate the nature of the classroom management challenge, the teachers set up a group of three metrics, and data was gathered. These three metrics are easy to track and daily data was collected for two to three weeks, a total of forty-four classroom days.

1. Multiple requests to follow directions
2. Failure to actively listen
3. Bad attitude/conflict

Loss of Instruction Time

Two items of data are needed to quantify instructional lost time:

1. How often does a disruption occur?
2. Once the classroom is disrupted, how long does it take to return to the normal instructional mode?

Dealing with the number one first leads to interesting and very important concepts.

As the teachers contemplated these estimates, discussion targeted the framework in which the teachers should position their thinking. The classroom has settled down, and the entire classroom is in an instructional mode, that is, in the "learning groove." Suddenly there is an outburst of anger by one of the students. Everything stops, the students raise their heads to listen and observe the disruption; the teacher immediately leaves instructional mode and enters a disciplinary mode.

Minutes later the disruption seems to be over and the students go back to work. Are the students at this point truly able to focus on learning, or is more time going to pass before the class is truly back into an instructional mode. The teachers were asked to estimate the time from the beginning of the disturbance to the return of the apparent instructional mode. Certainly, off the cuff, this is not easy to do. However, estimates were made and subsequently used to estimate the minutes of classroom time lost each day to interruptions.

The illustrations below are another way to visualize lost time estimates. The disturbance is over when the last ripple is gone.

Figure 4.3.

Figure 4.4.

Figure 4.3 is a picture that depicts a classroom that is interrupted by a single event. Learning in this classroom will be somewhat impaired by wasted teacher time, but disturbances like this would be quite common.

Figure 4.4 illustrates a case of many ongoing small disturbances; the ripples do not go away leading to a period of constant disruption.

Lastly, figure 4.5 depicts a major disciplinary problem. This could be a violent outburst or a fight. In this case, the ripples turn to waves, and the impact on the entire class is very severe.

Disruptions of this magnitude take a long time to get over and may leave mental scars that last for hours or even days.

Table 4.8 shows the time estimates the teachers selected for the duration of each of the three types of classroom disruptions.

Now what is needed is the average daily count for each disruption type. Using clipboards and tally marks, the teachers made these estimates. The data in table 4.9 was gathered over forty-four classroom days (all four teachers).

Figure 4.5.

Table 4.8. Teacher's Estimates of the Length of a Disruption

Measured Disruption	Instructional Time Lost in Minutes per Event
Multiple requests to follow directions	0.5
Failure to actively listen	0.25
Bad attitude/conflict	4.5

Table 4.9.   Daily Average Distractions for Typical Classroom. The Total Tally Marks Are Averaged per Day per Class

	Multiple Requests to Follow Directions	Failure to Actively Listen	Bad Attitude/Conflict
Overall average	26	11	10

Table 4.10.   How Much Time Is Lost Each Day to Classroom Disruptions?

Measured Disruption	Time Loss per Event	Average Number of Events per Day	Total in Minutes
Multiple requests to follow directions	0.5	26	13
Failure to actively listen	0.25	11	3
Bad attitude/conflict	4.5	10.23	46
Total lost time for each classroom each day			62

To find the total average lost instructional time per day, simply multiply the duration of the event by the number of times it occurs per day. Table 4.10 shows the results of this multiplication; the result is 62 minutes of lost time each day.

How important is the lost 62 minutes per day? Appendix C, page 141, Table C.1 shows how the teachers spend their time in a typical day. There are 420 minutes at school (7 hours); subtracting lunches, recess, etc. leaves 220 minutes of instruction by the teacher. The out of classroom instruction of 60 minutes is under the control of the music teacher, art teacher, etc. so it is not included in the 220 minutes. Dividing 62 minutes by 220 minutes gives a 28% loss; a loss that no student can afford. This is 186 hours on an annual basis.

TEXT BOX 4.9

Each day, in each classroom, the teacher must deal with 62 minutes of lost instructional time, 46 minutes of which comes from disciplinary issues.

This lost time is one of the major reasons more of these students did not do well on their assessment exams, especially with the teachers saying they have the ability to be successful.

As extra supporting information, a highly respected retired principal of two elementary schools in Lawrence Township, Indianapolis, Indiana reviewed this estimation process and made this comment: "The 62 minutes of lost instructional time is too low."

Suppose it was possible to suddenly snap our fingers and convert all *disruptive* students into engaged. This group of five to six students account for thirty-seven minutes of the total of sixty-two minutes. Not only would we pick up the thirty-seven minutes, we would see a dramatic improvement in the remaining twenty-five minutes since the *followers* are no longer influenced by the *disruptives*.

Since *engaged* students need very little classroom management (0.9 minutes), the teacher would be able to recoup most of the 220 minutes of instructional time with the students. (Note in appendix D that the teachers do not count the sixty minutes of out-of-class instructional time. This is music, art, or computer instruction done by another teacher. Any misbehavior in these classes leads to an immediate return of the offending students to their regular classroom.)

This improved time availability, along with a much-improved learning environment, will provide the impetus needed to excel on the standardized exams. The teachers believe that this is one of the primary root causes for the classes' poor test performance. There is also a major psychological consideration that will be beneficial. The engaged and the follower students are amenable to learning. What are they thinking about their desire to learn when the teacher and the administration allow so much disruption and loss of time in the classroom?

TEXT BOX 4.10

It is not allowed for one student to interfere in the education of another.

Inculcating this motto into a school's set of habits could have a big impact if is truly supported by all involved.

LOOKING FOR ROOT CAUSE

It would be easy to stop at this point and simply find someone to blame but this would be stopping too early in our quest for the root cause. The question is why the disruptive students are unruly and create such a problem in class? The teachers agree that they do not possess certain socioemotional and the motivation skills that are usually taken for granted, and if they do have the appropriate skills, they are hiding them while in the classroom.

Here is the list of skills the teachers say the *disruptive* students are lacking:

- The understanding that education is essential for them to lead a better life.
- The understanding that even though their circumstances may be far from ideal, they can still be successful if they believe in their teachers and their role in teaching them essential skills.
- They need to understand why respect of others is so essential for their own success.
- They need to learn how to manage the behaviors that are brought about because of their life situation.
- They need to understand the importance of self-discipline and self- motivation.
- They need to understand what language is acceptable and what is profane and unacceptable.
- They need to understand how to deal with conflict and how to avoid inflicting either mental or physical harm upon others.
- They need to learn the virtue of perseverance and its importance—learning can be hard work.

The High-Level Attributes of Character and Grit

In chapter 3, the idea and the importance of character and grit were introduced. At that time, the seven higher-level attributes of character and grit were listed. For convenience, they are repeated here:

1. Curiosity
2. Gratitude
3. Zest
4. Optimism
5. Self-control
6. Social intelligence
7. Grit

Each of the skills the teachers say the *disruptive* students are lacking can be positioned under one of these higher-level attributes. This is the basis for the conclusion that they are lacking in character and grit.

Remember that life skills are learned just like knowledge skills. These skills are taken for granted because children usually learn them a little at a time over many years; skills they are taught by the people who raise them, or neighbors, coaches, teachers, and friends. So, the teachers report that there is a major shortfall in these skills that need to be addressed. Is it too early to expect fourth graders to be able to change behavior? The teachers don't think so. It would be very beneficial to the student, future classrooms, and society if they could gain more successful noncognitive skills earlier in their lives.

Here is an area of their growth reserved for the "educational experts" to comment upon and set a plan in place that will be of major benefit to all concerned. One thing is for sure: it will not be easy to get these children to recognize their deficiencies nor to spend the time to remedy them.

The Students Are Lacking Character and Grit

What is needed is an approach that will provide the skills for these students to live in two different worlds. In addition to their current circumstance, they need the basic skills to allow them to succeed in the world of the classroom; these are talents that will hold them in good stead in the later years in education, business and governmental jobs, and the military.

As the reader can understand, these are not the ordinary pursuits of a conventionally trained teacher nor a typical school. Typical school knowledge is not all that these students need at this point.

The Root Causes—The Last Why

"Why don't the *disruptive* students possess the needed noncognative skills to be successful in the classroom?" The teachers produced this list:

1. *Parents/parenting*—their parents have not imparted to them the needed noncognitive skills or the motivation to become better educated.
2. *Cultural*—there are cultural biases in some ethnic groups that do not admire and sometime denigrate intellectual capabilities.
3. *Choice*—the students have made the choice to be uncooperative and to produce disruption in the classroom.

The most important root cause by far is the parents/parenting. If this could be fixed, the other two would probably be insignificant. Our four teachers bristle when they talk about the *disruptive* students' parents. The teachers do not have that many options beyond their own classroom management skills, which do not work on their *disruptive* students, so not having parents to help is a major loss.

Here Is a Speech Relevant to Point 2 Above

Here is a portion of Michelle Obama's 2013 Commencement Address at Bowie State University[13], Prince George's County, Maryland, it was a twenty- to twenty-five-minute address.

> But today, more than 150 years after the Emancipation Proclamation, more than 50 years after the end of "separate but equal," when it comes to getting an education, too many of our young people just can't be bothered. Today, instead of walking miles every day to school, they're sitting on couches for hours playing video games, watching TV. Instead of dreaming of being a teacher or a lawyer or a business leader, they're fantasizing about being a baller or a rapper. (Applause.) Right now, one in three African American students are dropping out of high school. Only one in five African Americans between the ages of 25 and 29 has gotten a college degree—one in five.
>
> It is that kind of unwavering determination—that relentless focus on getting an education in the face of obstacles—that's what we need to reclaim, as a community and as a nation. That was the idea at the very heart of the founding of this school.
>
> So I think we can agree, and we need to start feeling that hunger again, you know what I mean? (Applause.) We need to once again fight to educate ourselves and our children like our lives depend on it, because they do.

A CONFIRMING STUDY

At this point, it has been shown that a number of children (23 percent for this study) are so difficult to manage that they are causing, either directly or indirectly, a loss of sixty-two minutes each day in each classroom. Of these sixty-two minutes, forty-six minutes are due to attitude and discipline.

After much research looking for studies like this one, nothing even close has been uncovered. In addition, a professional expert on education is also unaware of any similar project; this expert was engaged to assist in the early phases of this project. There is one report that is related, but its results were obtained by a different process. It finds similar results regarding misbehaving children, but by using surveys and consequently has no quantification of percentage of students and lost classroom time.

In May 2004 Public Agenda published a report entitled: *Teaching Interrupted, Do Discipline Policies in Today's Public Schools Foster the Common Good?* Here is material from their website to tell us who they are.[14]

> *Public Agenda is a nonprofit, nonpartisan organization that helps diverse leaders and citizens navigate divisive, complex issues and work together to find solutions.*

Through nonpartisan research and public engagement, we provide the insights, tools, and support people needed to build common ground and arrive at solutions that work for them. In doing so, we are proving that it is possible to make progress on critical issues regardless of our differences.

They say, in all their work, they seek to help build a democracy in which problem solving triumphs over gridlock and inertia, and where public policy reflects the thoughtful input and values of the nation's citizens. Public Agenda was founded by social scientist and author Daniel Yankelovich and former secretary of state Cyrus Vance in 1975. They work to help leaders and citizens move toward solutions on a variety of issues.

Their study relied on a national random sample of 725 middle and high school teachers and 600 parents of middle and high school students. The surveys provide a detailed look at the discipline issue, looking for its causes, the effectiveness of current policies, and the impact on school climate and receptivity to various solutions.

Information from *Teaching Interrupted*'s Their Executive Summary

These findings confirm that research previously discussed illustrates a problem that exists throughout the nation.[15] Many of their results are presented since this study is so relevant to this book and because their findings are so important.

"The vast majority of both teachers (85%) and parents (73%) say that the school experience of most students suffers at the expense of a few chronic offenders."

"Most teachers (78%) report that students who are persistent behavior problems should be removed from the school grounds but are not removed."

"Too many students are losing critical opportunities for learning—and too many teachers are leaving the profession—because of a few persistent trouble-makers. What's more, say teachers, today's misbehaving students are quick to remind them that students have rights and their parents can sue."

Here are some of the additional study conclusions that are relevant to this book:

"Nearly half (49%) of the teachers complain they have been accused of unfairly disciplining a student."

"More than half (55%) say that districts backing down from assertive parents causes discipline problems."

"It's almost unanimously accepted among teachers (98%) that a school needs good discipline and behavior to flourish, and 78% of parents agree."

"It is also widely accepted among both groups that part of a school's mission—in addition to teaching the three R's—is to teach kids to follow the rules so they can become productive citizens (teachers 93% and parents 88%)."

"Students pay a heavy price academically when schools tolerate the chronic bad behavior of the few. Most teachers (77%) admit their teaching would be a lot more effective if they didn't have to spend so much time dealing with disruptive students."

Look at some of the report's root causes for the problems in today's schools

Topping the list of causes of behavior problems in the nation's schools is parents' failure to teach their children discipline (teachers 82% and parents 74%).

Second on the list is: There's disrespect everywhere in our culture—students absorb it and bring it to school (73% and 68%). Other Public Agenda research shows that *only about a third of parents* say they have succeeded in teaching their children to have self-control and discipline, while half say they have succeeded in teaching their child to do their best in school.

Dealing with persistent troublemakers

Seventy percent of teachers and 68% of parents strongly support the establishment of "zero tolerance" policies so students know they will be kicked out of school for various violations, with another 23% of teachers and 20% of parents indicating they support this idea somewhat (Total support 93% teachers and 89% parents).

In addition, 46% of teachers and 33% of parents strongly support giving principals a lot more authority to handle discipline issues as they see fit, with another 33% of teachers and 73% of parents supporting this idea somewhat (Total support: 84% teachers; 74% parents).

Putting more responsibility on parents

A strong majority of teachers (69%) say finding ways to hold parents more accountable for kids' behavior would be a very effective solution to the schools' discipline problems.

Limiting lawsuits on discipline

Forty-two percent of teachers and 46% of parents strongly support limiting lawsuits to serious situations like expulsion, with another 40% of teachers and 32% of parents liking this idea somewhat (Total support: 82% teachers; 78% parents).

Fifty percent of teachers and 43% of parents also strongly approve of removing the possibility of monetary awards for parents who sue over discipline issues (Total support: 82% teachers; 69% parents).

Comments on This Report

This report goes further than the school research in that it includes the issue of lawsuits. The teachers never mentioned a fear of being sued in all the team's discussions. Otherwise, it too reports, just as has been explained in this book, that a percentage of troublemakers are costing classroom time and causing teachers to leave the profession.

What is surprising is the high percentage of the public, in this instance parents, who know about these issues. This report was released in May of 2004, and it does not seem as though it had much impact. Hours and hours of research focused on misbehaving students and lost classroom time never discovered a single reference to *Teaching Interrupted*. Luckily it was discovered because it establishes the national scope of the classroom problem. Here again, the absolute reluctance of professional educators to, in any way, associate themselves with work blaming students for the problems in many classrooms.

In the current environment, to do this "one off" would probably cost them their jobs. The public just do not want to hear this argument; in their eyes, it's the teacher's job to manage the classroom. Generally, this would not be an unreasonable expectation but in today's world, a percentage of the children around the country are not manageable by the majority of teachers.

Given the current trends, these problems will not be resolved before there is a major crisis in the teaching profession brought about by the fact that too few young people want to devote their lives to teaching. This trend has already started and is well on its way.

Chapter 5

Looking for a Solution

MOTIVATION—WHAT DOESN'T WORK AND WHAT DOES?

A common "solution" for supposedly bad schools is to incentivize teachers with bonuses and other monetary rewards. This section shows that this just doesn't work; assuming the pay is not *too low*, teachers are motived by intrinsic rewards, not extrinsic.

What Doesn't Work—Very Important

Ronald Fryer is a professor of economics at Harvard University. He has spent an extensive amount of time and vast sums of money hoping to find a motivational stimulus from financial incentives. Between 2007 and 2009, he distributed a total of $9.4 million dollars to 27,000 *students* in Chicago, Dallas, and New York City. Of this experiment, he says:

> "The results from our incentive experiments on student achievement are surprising." "The impact of financial incentives on student achievement is statistically 0 in each city."[1]

During 2007 and 2010, Professor Fryer oversaw and evaluated a program jointly administered by New York City's education department and the teacher's union that distributed $75 million in cash to the city's lowest performing schools. He reports:

> I find no evidence that teacher incentives increase student performance, attendance or graduation; nor do I find evidence that incentives change student or teacher behavior. If anything, teacher incentives may decrease student achievement, especially in large schools.[2]

These findings fly in the face of programs around the country to install performance-based incentive programs to reward the "best" teachers. Apparently, they are best because that have an internal mission to change student lives as opposed to maximizing their income. If this deduction is correct, it is imperative that school administrators establish discipline and support systems to allow the teachers to do their jobs.

A Recent Action to Reward Teachers in Indiana

The Indiana legislature set aside $40 million to reward the better teachers for their efforts. Recently these funds were awarded and the Indianapolis Star wrote an article entitled: *Teachers Bonus Pay Favors Rich Districts*.[3] The article pointed out how teachers in the Carmel Clay and Zionsville school (both systems are in high-income areas) district receive $2,422 and $2,239, respectively, while teachers with the same performance rating in the Indianapolis Public School system will receive $128 and Wayne Township will receive only $42/teacher.

The Indianapolis-based website, www.elevateteachers.org, recently featured this topic in a blog written by the author.

WEALTHY SCHOOL DISTRICT TEACHERS
RECEIVE HIGHER BONUSES

The Indianapolis Star recently published an article pointing out the disparity in teacher performance pay in wealthy school districts versus low-income school districts in Indiana. According to data from the Indiana Department of Education, *most* teachers (those rated highly effective or effective) at Carmel Clay Schools and Zionsville Community Schools will receive over $2,200 in performance money. However, Indianapolis Public Schools teachers with the same ratings will receive only $128 per teacher; similarly, teachers in Wayne Township Schools will see the lowest payments at $42 per teacher.

"What it does do is channel even more money to those school corporations that already get the largest slices of the financial pie," says House Democratic leader Scott Pelath, a Michigan City Democrat whose local school district received none of the funding.

Though supporters of the money say it's intended to reward good teachers, House Speaker Brian Bosma and Superintendent-elect Jennifer McCormick both say they think lawmakers should review the performance-based pay. According to Teresa Meredith, president of the Indiana State Teachers Association, this payment rewards schools with access to better resources and supports, while poorer schools get less—or nothing.

Elevate Teachers founder Richard Garrett thinks the disparity in payments is outrageous, because teachers at wealthier schools don't have the same challenges as those at low-income schools. "This system of allocation must be changed! The morale of the low-income teachers is already bad and this is a terrible slap in the face to them all," Garrett said.

This distribution of incentive pay was a major blunder. Based on what Professor Fryer's research just reported, incentive pay is not working in the first place. The teachers in the wealthy districts just happened to be in the right place at the right time. Most certainly, the wealthy districts have *disruptive* students, but their behavior and numbers will be far less of a teaching issue than those in the low-income areas.

Garrett continues to say this bonus pay allocation scheme was a slap in the face for teachers in low-income areas. *The Indianapolis Star* published this article on December 22, 2016—seven days after the original announcement article. *Teachers make the most of "insult."*[4]

The story points out that some of the best teachers in Wayne Township will not accept their $42 bonus, and it explains how the paltry check discourages teaching in disadvantaged districts. It is a representation of how the Indiana legislators feel about their work with children affected by poverty and hardship. The teachers call for an even distribution for effective teachers across the state without regard for their school district. If this had been done, each teacher rated effective or highly effective would have received approximately $600.

If Money Won't Work, What Will?

Here is an important answer to explain motivation that was initially formulated in the 1970s by professors Edward Deci and Richard Ryan from the University of Rochester:[5]

> Deci and Ryan, by contrast, argued that we are mostly motivated not by the material consequences of our actions, but by the inherent enjoyment and meaning those actions bring us, a phenomenon they labeled intrinsic motivation. They identified three key human needs—our need for competence, our need for autonomy, and our need for relatedness, meaning personal connection. And they contended that intrinsic motivation can be sustained only when we feel that those needs are being satisfied.

Dwell a moment on the terms competence, autonomy, and relatedness since understanding them is critical to understanding this definition of intrinsic motivation.

1. Competence—Seek to control the outcome and experience mastery. He is a competent musician; she is a competent systems analyst.

2. Autonomy—

    a. Universal urge to be in control of one's life and act in harmony with one's integrated self; however, note this does not mean to be independent of others.

    b. Freedom from external control or influence, independence; e.g. An independent business person has a great deal of autonomy.

3. Relatedness—universal desire to interact, be connected to, and experience caring from others. Examples—a member of a family, a class at school, a team, and so on.

In the context of this book, this concept applies to both teachers and students.

Testing If Model Works for Students

Think about students who attend or participate in the five successful organizations selected later in this chapter. In chapter 4, the conclusion is drawn that the kids are smart enough. This says that under the right circumstances (which exist in the "success story" schools), children complete high school and many go on to college or to vocational jobs. This means they develop competence in their studies; these five organizations meet the first criteria. Next is autonomy. In these organizations, they place great emphasis on knowing these children as individuals. They will work with them individually if it is required to help them keep pace. They teach values that apply to them individually.

Lastly is relatedness. This is one of their great strengths. In their classrooms, the children know each other, rely on each other, and support each other. In addition, The Oaks Academy is very popular and many children and teachers want to go here. They are successful because they meet the criteria to intrinsically motivate each student. Looking at the teachers, we see individuals who are high on the teacher's emotional bank account scale (see chapter 4). They love their jobs; they are changing lives; they are receiving ample quantities of intrinsic motivation. Happy teachers produce happy children.

Does the Deci and Ryan Model Work for Teachers?

A few paragraphs above we learned that money (extrinsic motivation) is not a big motivator for teachers. Certainly, the salaries need to be a living wage but most of a teacher's motivation is intrinsic. Again, Deci and Ryan say that three needs must be met for intrinsic motivation. Again, these are:

1. Competence
2. Autonomy
3. Relatedness.

Point 2. All teachers have at least four years of undergraduate training, and many hold a master's degree. So, point 2 is a yes. Do teachers have autonomy? Absolutely not, their profession is one of the most unempowered professions in America. So, point 1 is a no. Point 3 is relatedness. Do teachers experience caring from others? They certainly do from other teachers but society in general, no. They are pounded by the press and blamed for many of the ills of education.

Since all three needs need to be met for intrinsic motivation, it is no surprise that teachers' morale is at a record low and that their status is not high. Using the idea of the emotional bank account, they are overdrawn on their emotional balance; they are in negative territory. So, the Deci and Ryan model works, but this time it predicts an unmotivated person.

A LOGICAL PLACE TO FIND HELP

Normally it is not productive to dwell on things tried that did not work, but this was so logically appealing that it was decided to include it in the book. In chapter 4, there is a list of 114 high-poverty public schools in Indiana that received a school grade of A. These schools seem to have found the keys to success since all of them are in districts with free and reduced lunch percentages greater than 70 percent.

In June 2016, twenty-six letters were sent to the principals of some of the most impoverished schools. The letter congratulated them for their outstanding accomplishments and for finding a teaching method that worked with high-poverty children. The entire list of 114 schools was included in the letter to illustrate this public school success. Further the letter pointed out that they should be lauded for their success.

Obviously, they were employing "best practices." What were they doing that could be incorporated into this book and passed on to other schools? Unfortunately, there was not a single reply to the letters. Perhaps, if this book proves to be a success, another book can be written about "best practices" (yea, a sequel!).

WHAT SHOULD BE DONE?

Here's the book's posture at this point:

TEXT BOX 5.1

It is terribly wrong for this group of disruptive students to deprive the balance of the class, students who are amenable to education, from an opportunity to learn and excel.

OPTION 1: MAKE NO CHANGES

One option is to continue without any change. This means everything assessed continues, and 77 percent of the students in the class will not reach their potential. How must they feel when they continually experience the interruptions from the *disruptive* students? Since the school system seems to pay little or no attention to dealing with the *disruptive* students to modify their behavior, the remaining children realize they are being written off since they do not receive enough quality instruction time. They will continue to do poorly on the state exams, and they will see themselves as failed students.

Another thing to consider is the loss of self-confidence. Despite your intellectual level, if personal progress is not being made, a lack of confidence sets in and school turns into an unhappy, discouraging place. Learning is its own reward.

Recall presidential candidate Ben Carson's story about his mother and her reading assignments and how she required a written report on each book. He was required to read books and write reports that his mother graded. Little did he know that his mother could not read—not only books but also his written reports. By the time he figured this out, he was so in love with reading that from that point on he was a self-propelled learner. This is a situation where learning is its own reward.

OPTION 2: CHANGE CLASS STRUCTURE

Much time and much research have gone to answer the question, "Can these disruptive students be turned around and made into productive citizens?" In the literature, there is documentation about what doesn't happen to many of these children in the first five years of their life. Supposedly their intellectual capacity has been defined and their brains programmed but at levels inferior to more affluent children—children who have experienced substantial stimulation in their early years.

This may be the case, but many positive things can still be accomplished. The teachers, not just the four involved in this research but most of the thirty plus educators who critiqued the research, support the contention that these students have the intellectual capabilities to pass the state exams; a statement that does not consider what happened to them in their first five years of life.

As has been stated, they are lacking in character and grit. These are teachable skills. Many schools, like the 114 on our Hit Parade of Schools, have learned how to do it; personal dialogue with teachers who know how to do it has occurred, sports participation can do it, the U.S. Marines do it, Geoffrey Canada of the Harlem Children's Zone does it, and many others. There are just too many counter examples that bring these children into line with more affluent children to deny the likelihood of success.

Move the Disruptive Students to a Separate class

Just like the report reviewed from Public Agenda, it is recommended that the disruptive students be removed from the classroom. They will not be "written off" but be placed in an environment that will expand upon what they learn and how they do it. They need a different mix of instruction, one rich in non-cognitive skills as well as cognitive skills.

In the case of the four fourth grades we have been studying, there are a total of 4 × 24 students, or 96 total. Twenty-three percent of these are

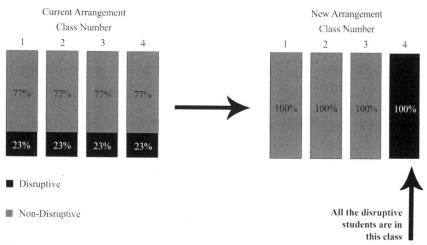

Figure 5.1. Arrangement of disruptive students.

disruptive students so a class of twenty-two *disruptives* is established and three classes of twenty-four to twenty-five others, the *engaged* and the *followers*, this is pictured in figure 5.1.

Here is a pictorial representation to illustrate the new configuration:
Here are the six essentials for the new class 4:

1. Emphasizes/teaches character and grit.
2. Utilizes discipline as a teaching tool.
3. Values are taught and ingrained into all students.
4. Provides an environment of fellowship and camaraderie—something they are missing at home.
5. Has a substantial amount of caring adult intervention.
6. Continues to teach the required course material.

The new class will probably need to be taught by two caring adults who have the experience and talent to manage this difficult class. Since the restoration of hope in a child is keyed to the presence of caring adults, two caring adults will do a better job.

Another important feature of this configuration is that the other three classes can be taught by "ordinary" teachers who do not have to waste valuable minutes of instructional time maintaining order. This will boost staff morale for these individuals. If something like this is not done, it is going to be very difficult to hire any teaching staff, particularly considering what we said in chapter 2.

Listen to an Expert—An Experienced Teacher Who Can Do It Alone

Several years ago, after bringing up an earlier website with the address: www.failingschool.org, contact was made with an experienced teacher who taught difficult children in inner city schools of Houston, Texas. Within the past few months, this contact was revived as content was needed for this book. The teaching profession does not have many teachers with skills to teach the *disruptive* students. Ms. Minyon can do this job; hopefully her advice will assist other teachers.

Her name is Janice Minyon, and she has an interesting background. She is a sumna cum laude graduate of the University of Pittsburg with a major in education and is incredibly serious about teaching. She has worked many years in education but not all of it was in a classroom, for example, she worked for Johns Hopkins for six years advocating for their reading program across the nation.

In her first year of teaching, she willingly accepted the responsibility to teach a grade exactly like class 4 in the diagram above, see figure 5.1- the class on the far right; she wanted the challenge of working with these children so badly in need of an education. She willingly did this for eighteen years and felt a great deal of satisfaction with her success. Not a single child she taught was beyond her patience or her ability to teach. She produced successful students. Her teaching is yet another example of the hope talked about in this book. These students can learn!

After numerous telephone conversations, one thing is apparent that she has outstanding diagnostic skills and can come up with teaching techniques that overcome the deficiencies of the approach normally used in schools. She applies her great intellectual skills where they are needed, in the classroom. She has a complete set of her personal documentation of how to teach in general, and how to best teach different topics.

She is attempting to sell this material to school districts, but she was good enough to produce, for this book, her top ten best ideas to teach elementary children, including some twelve- and thirteen-year-old fourth-grade students not yet able to read nor compute any mathematics.

TOP-TEN BEST IDEAS OF AN EXPERIENCED TEACHER

Basic to these ten points is a strategy to maximize learning and to minimize discipline problems. At the beginning of the school year, the students are placed on two person teams. It is identical to picking teams, for example, for the NCAA basketball playoffs. Put the best student with the worst student, the next best with the next worst, and so on. Here are some of the advantages:

1. The better students benefit from helping the weaker students in that they explain concepts, provide assistance with reading, and so on. This help reinforces their skills.
2. The weaker students benefit from hearing their peer explain ideas; the uptake here is in the range of 69 percent, which is considerably above the retention from a lecture (in the range of 6 percent). In addition, advice from the partner can be repeated whenever needed.
3. Questions, complements, and admonitions are aimed at the team and not an individual. This calling on the team, shelters individual students from bad recognition, one of her important goals; all students dread negative attention.

This may look like a one-way street with information and insights only moving from the brighter student to the team mate but this is not the case; it will be a two-way street.

THE TEN POINTS

1. Build self-esteem. The key is to make the student feel successful. Chapter 3 explains that learning character and grit will build self-esteem; these skills, along with progress in demonstrating knowledge gained, will make the student feel successful. This point is at the head of the list because it is, by far, the most important item.

2. Everything is reading; spelling is reading, language is reading, science and social studies is reading, and so on. It is required that the students exhibit reading skills in all topics.

3. Science—use experiments to teach science. Ms. Minyon says that a student "would walk five miles in the snow if they knew a science lesson was going to be a hands-on experiment."

4. Never skip spelling or language. Young children at this age can pronounce many words, but many times they do not know the meaning of the words. Spelling not only produces the proper sequence of letters but it adds words to their vocabulary.

5. Math is the easiest to teach. The essence of teaching math is to move knowledge from short-term to long-term memory. Every day, before the math lesson, the students work on ten problems they have already seen— maybe not the exact same problem but similar. This repeat work helps to lodge the older knowledge in long-term memory. Classroom grades are only given to individual students; teams are not graded.

6. Only reward students for *wanted* behavior. Do not publicly recognize their negatives. Reward a team of students when something good happens. Calling out a student's name for bad behavior gives the student recognition for the wrong reason. If a student is misbehaving, she will stand by his or her side with a stern look on her face and if that does not work, she whispers for him or her to behave.

7. Spelling tests. Every Friday the students are given the weekly spelling test. On Thursday, the teacher gives a spelling pretest on the words that will be on the Friday exam. If a student receives a 100 percent on the Thursday pretest, they do not have to take the Friday exam; they are free to do whatever they want (quietly) during the Friday exam.

8. When reading something short and low level, as an example, *The Three Little Pigs*, ask questions that develop higher-level learning—questions that go well beyond the story itself.

9. Model handwriting. If writing on the board, let them watch the writing. If writing on an overhead, let them see the writing take place.

10. On Friday, the teachers celebrate the successes of the week. The teachers give themselves a pat on the back. They tell the students to enjoy their weekend, and they, the teachers, come to class on Monday with smiles and enthusiasm.

Turn the Classroom into a Family

After much reading, looking at several programs, some of which will be discussed later, this is concluded: turn the *disruptive* student classroom into a family.

TEXT BOX 5.2

Turn the classroom into a family.

A key need is to bond these students into a cohesive unit, a social unit that will, to some degree, serve as the family they need so badly. This happens in the movie *Freedom Writers*, and it can be seen at the St. Benedictine Prep School in Newark, New Jersey as well.[6] This happens in Elevate America. It happens at the Shepherd Community Center that serves the east side of Indianapolis and the Oaks Academy located in a lower-income area in the near north side of Indianapolis.

How do the teachers bond the students to each other? Time is spent letting the students talk about their lives, their experiences, relatives and friends lost through conflict, their family situation, and so on. They will find that they have much in common, and this can lead to a natural association. This suggests a short story read as a young student, *Adversity Builds Bonds*. These students have much adversity and should bond up in most cases.

In addition to the usual school topics, the teachers need to teach character and develop programs to build perseverance/grit. It will probably take at least two teachers to manage these classes. One will focus on the traditional curriculum, and the other will focus on bonding the class into a cohesive unit and teaching character and grit.

Going to the St. Benedictine model, the new students go on a fifty-three-mile hike along with upper classmen. This is not a typical boot camp but a team- and grit-building experience. They encourage each other, they show love for each other, and they teach character as they interact with each other. In St. Benedictine's case, the students play a major role in managing their school.

In designing this program, bring in some carefully selected upper-class students to act as the leaders. (This is what Elevate USA does.) This would be a win-win action for both the selected students as well as the class itself. The adults would stand at the side and work with the selected leaders to let them manage the program in a positive way.

Like The Oaks Academy discussed above, values must be developed, marketed, and lived each day. To ingrain these values will take constant repetition and full organizational support.

This type of program would be ideal for a summer school session so that the students don't fall behind the school calendar too far.

Here is a writing from Cynthia J. Johnson[7]

> Seven ways to connect to and validate children who live in poverty:
> Establish a caring and believing environment.
> Get to know each student's name.
> Determine what each student is interested in.
> Survey students to learn about family and daily practices.
> Identify students' learning styles.
> Allow students to "tell" their story.
> Build lessons based on information learned about the students in your class.

These are some of the steps a teacher takes to turn the classroom into a family.

TEACH DISCIPLINE

This is going to be a somewhat unusual approach to the subject of discipline. Schools need to view discipline just like they view math and reading; it is another topic that must be taught. This book, with its great emphasis on the importance of character and grit, argues that, because of shortfalls in many families, discipline is not being taught at home.

In many family situations, it would be foolhardy to take a position that discipline falls into the responsibilities of the parents and they must "shape up" and do a better job; it is not the domain of the schools. The probability of changing parental behavior, if it is not now happening, is very low. Consequently, if successful children are going to be produced, values must be taught at school.

Discipline is a great way to teach character and grit. Teaching discipline is a win-win proposition. The teachers win when the classroom behaviors improve, and they end up with more instructional time—this outcome will make positive deposits into their emotional bank accounts. The students win because learning discipline and the associated improvements in character and grit will boost their self-esteem. They also have emotional bank accounts and their balances will go from negative to positive.

They will receive more instruction time and they will begin to see that they have the talent to make better grades. This establishment of competency will improve their intrinsic motivation. It is an upward spiral that has been demonstrated over and over again in schools throughout America.

THE POWER OF EARLY EDUCATION—GET STARTED EARLY

There is a growing commitment to training children in their early years—generally stated as pre-K training (meaning pre-kindergarten). Financially, the trend in state spending on early education has a definite upward slope. In 2014–2015 state spending topped $6.2 billion, an increase of over $553 million over the previous year, although two-thirds of this increase can be attributed to New York.

Spending per child saw the largest increase in a decade, reaching $4,489 per child (pre-K). State-funded pre-K served almost 1.4 million children in 2014–2015, an increase of 37,167 children from the previous year. Funding in 2010 was $5.4 billion.[8] Putting this into perspective here is a comparison to other spending totals for 2014–2015 for different programs and different levels.

Figure 5.2 shows that the cost of pre-K spending, the lower three bars, is considerably lower than K–12 spending per student. The government's Head Start program seems way out of line.

Here is this book's starting position for early childhood training. Recall that in chapter 4, the teachers concluded the primary root cause for the *disruptive* children was:

Parents/parenting—their parents have not imparted to them the needed noncognitive skills or the motivation to become better educated.

TEXT BOX 5.3

Opinion: The only children that should be receiving government-funded pre-K schooling are children like the *disruptive* students. Recall that they are the very difficult to manage as they receive very little support from their parents; in fact shortfalls in parenting is a root cause for their behavioral problems in the classroom. Any training they receive should be rich in noncognitive skills along with cognitive. These students need self-management so they can be good classroom students later in their journey—they need character and grit!

Noncognitive skills is a more sophisticated name for character and grit. It is the absence of these skills that get the students into trouble as they advance in the school system. Their deficiencies are in large part the root cause of many of the problems in the teaching profession such as teacher recruitment,

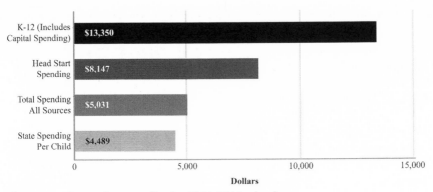

Figure 5.2.   Per student spending for 2014–2015 school year.

teacher retention, teacher burnout, and so on. There is no substitute for these skills being imparted by one or more parents but, in lieu of that, they will have to come from the school system.

James Heckman says:[9]

> "When preschool programs have been evaluated, the effects are biggest for the most disadvantaged children," Heckman said. By contrast, preschool has negligible effects on middle-class kids. "A lot of those kids are already getting enriched early childhood environments."

Early Childhood Education Literature

The early childhood education literature is filled with articles like this:[10]

> "The emotional, social and physical development of young children has a direct effect on their overall development and on the adult they will become. That is why understanding the need to invest in very young children is so important, so as to maximize their future well-being."
>
> "Neurological research shows that the early years play a key role in children's brain development. Babies begin to learn about the world around them from a very early age—including during the prenatal, perinatal (immediately before and after birth) and postnatal period."
>
> "Children's early experiences—the bonds they form with their parents and their first learning experiences—deeply affect their future physical, cognitive, emotional and social development. Optimizing the early years of children's lives is the best investment we can make as a society in ensuring their future success."

Paul Tough writes:[11] "Still, there is overwhelming evidence that early childhood—the years before a child's sixth birthday, and especially before her third,—is a remarkable time of both opportunity and peril in a child's development."

Quotations like these are found throughout the literature that focuses on early childhood development.

Two Sides to the Argument

With this knowledge of the importance of early childhood stimulation, and with parents that fall short of their duties, *how can anyone believe that pre-K training will not be productive?* Surprisingly there are two sides to this argument:

1. Investing in early childhood education pays big dividends for years in the future.
2. There is insufficient good evidence to support the contention that early childhood investment pays off after the third grade.

How can any two positions be so far apart with early education appearing to be a straightforward and common sense need? Here are arguments on both sides of this issue.

RECENT INDIANA DEBATE ON PRE-K SPENDING

This is taken from a story in the Indianapolis Star.[12] Former Governor Mike Pence of Indiana had hoped that the states preschool program would receive funding from the federal government. He is now pushing for this program independent of any federal government assistance. Oddly enough, his support has opened old wounds as to the value of such programs.

The debated issue is whether the children receive any long-term benefit from the expenditure of these funds. The early childhood supporters say that these programs are essential to the success of children both while in school and later in life. The critics say that the benefits of these programs are of limited duration and will disappear by the end of the third grade.

The Case for Pre-K Education

Looking at the research literature, the preponderance of writings supports early education. Here are several arguments from noted sources.

"Early intervention programs enrich adverse family environments. The largest effects of the early intervention programs are on noncognitive traits. Now, what do I mean by that? I mean perseverance, motivation, self-esteem, and hard work."[13]

"Cognitive and character skills work together as dynamic complements; they are inseparable. Skills beget skills. More motivated children learn more. Those who are more informed usually make wiser decisions."[14]

"The cognitive skills prized by the American educational establishment and measured by achievement tests are only part of what is required for success in life. Character skills are equally important determinants of wages, education, health and many other significant aspects of flourishing lives."[15]

More from Dr. Heckman, this time he deals with return on investment:[16]

And that, according to Heckman, makes preschool one of the most effective job-training programs out there. As evidence, he points to the Perry Preschool Project, an experiment done in the early 1960s in Ypsilanti, Michigan. Researchers took a bunch of 3- and 4-year-old kids from poor families and randomly assigned them to one of two groups. The kids in one group just lived their regular lives. And the kids in the other group went to preschool for two hours a day, five days a week.

After preschool, both groups went into the same regular Ypsilanti public school system and grew up side by side into adulthood.

Yet when researchers followed up with the kids as adults, they found huge differences. At age 27, the boys who had—almost two decades earlier—gone to preschool were now half as likely to be arrested and earned 50 percent more in salary that those who didn't.

And that wasn't all. At 27, girls who went to preschool were 50 percent more likely to have a savings account and 20 percent more likely to have a car. In general, the preschool kids got sick less often, were unemployed less often, and went to jail less often. Since then, many other studies have reported similar findings. These results made me think: What is going on in Preschool?

Table 5.1 is a summary of economic returns for three different long-term (longitudinal) studies.[17]

The worst benefit/cost ratio produces a return of 2.5 times the investment made in that educational program. The other two programs are many times better than the Abecedarian Project.

Here is a list of benefits from quality pre-K programs:[18]

Educational success and economic productivity

- Achievement test scores
- Special education and grade repetition
- High school graduation
- Behavior problems, delinquency, and crime

Table 5.1. Cost Benefit Ratios for Early Education Investments (in 2017 Dollars, 3 percent Discount Rate Used)

Program	Cost	Benefits	Benefit/Cost
Perry Pre-K (1960s Ypsilanti, MI, ages 3–4)	$24,361	$393,241	16
Chicago Child-Parent Centers (20 centers, ages 3–9)	$11,384	$115,598	10.2
Abecedarian Project (1972, Carolina—5 years long)	$97,861	$244,018	2.5

- Employment, earnings, and welfare dependency
- Smoking, drug use, and depression

Decreased costs to government

- Schooling costs
- Social services costs
- Crime costs
- Health care costs (teen pregnancy and smoking)

Here is one more study that confirms the finding already quoted.[19] There have been several economic-based studies of the benefits from early education, or pre-K. Art Rolnick and Rob Grunewald of the Minneapolis Federal Reserve Bank published a paper that estimates the returns (benefits) of investments in early education. They determined that, in terms of return on investment, early education yields a return that is superior to most Minnesota public projects that are justified by a return-on-investment criteria. The data about model programs, Perry Preschool for example, yields an $8 return for every $1 invested.

More results can be reported, but we have presented enough to prove the point—early education pays big dividends.

The Case against Pre-K Education

One of the more vocal voices urging caution in the use of public money for pre-K education is Grover J. "Russ" Whitehurst, senior fellow, Economic Studies, Center on Children and Families, Brookings Institute. He has a great deal of experience in educational research and cannot be easily dispatched.

Here is a summary of his conclusion to an in-depth study of thirteen pre-K studies.[20] There is no available evidence to allow a state government to make a large investment in establishing or expanding a pre-K program.

This does not necessarily imply that such investments should not take place since many tax dollars are spent on state parks, museums, sports facilities, and so on. These expenditures do not produce a quantifiable "return on the investment," but it is done nonetheless. All the Brookings Institute is trying to do is to enter the public debate to balance the argument by considering both sides of the argument.

The American Enterprise Institute just completed a 2016 report entitled: *Does Pre-K Work? The Research on Ten Early Childhood Programs—And What It Tells Us.*[21]

> The information provided by this body of research is less useful than commonly assumed. The research shows neither that "Pre-K works" nor that it does not, rather, it shows that some early childhood programs yield particular outcomes, sometimes, for some children. It shows that early childhood programs *can* have a significant, sustained impact on the lives of children born into disadvantaged circumstances. But, it falls short of showing that all programs have that impact.

This conclusion is both positive and negative. It says one must be very careful in the design and implementation of a pre-K program to be sure it is of sufficient quality and will obtain the results desired. If one is careful and insightful, good results can improve a child's life.

What's Going on Here?

How can there be such divergent conclusions? Common sense says that if a child who is deprived of proper parenting, almost any stimulus, training, and so on should have a positive impact. On the other hand, if the population in the programs includes students with proper parenting, the incremental benefit from spending time and money on these children will be minimal since most of their early education comes from their home. This is the missing variable—the quality of the parenting.

Another factor is the quality of the pre-K program. Many day-care centers that receive public funding claim to be a pre-K program when, in fact, all they do is "baby sit" the children while the parents work. Quality programs do produce results.

The last factor is the noncognitive learning these *disruptive* students need to be successful in school first grade and beyond. James Heckman, as presented by Paul Tough, argues that character and grit can be more important than knowledge skills. Is it possible to test/evaluate noncognitive skills? The answer is yes; Paul Tough talks about one school that gives routine rating on student progress. One way is to follow the students to see how they do in later life. Many of the early programs produced better citizens thereby yielding a great return on the investment.

SCHOOL SUCCESS STORIES

Are there existing school programs where a *disruptive* student can be success-ful? The answer is yes; there are many, many success stories in this country that have done great things with children in poverty. In the research study conducted with the four fourth grades, the *engaged* and the *followers* make up 77 percent of each class. If the programs we are describing pick students from this population, success is likely. If a program can only pick *disruptive* students, there will be more uncertainty in the outcome.

Five Case Studies

Here are some school stories that illustrate success with low-income children. Many of them illustrate how they turn the classroom into a family. Elevate USA is a prime example of turning the classroom into a family. The Oaks Academy places great emphasis on imparting values to their students—these examples are the kind of training provided by many parents.

ELEVATE USA

Here is an introduction to an in-school program that also works with high school students 24/7/365. They attend an Elevate class, just like they would an English class, and receive credit. The instructors are paid by Elevate. It was a pleasure to watch this class in action at Arsenal Technical High School in Indianapolis in the spring of 2016 then again in the fall of this same year.

The spring group had been together for the full semester and the students were well acquainted with each other, and they were engaged. Since this was one of the last classes of the semester, the focus was on having some fun by playing a little "get acquainted" game, and they treated me like a member of the class. The class was very enjoyable. This is an excellent example of turning the classroom into a family—this class was very close to being a "family"—for some of them much more meaningful than what they experience at home.

Introduction/Mission Statement

> *Transforming Cities by Building Long-Term Life-Changing Relationships with Urban Youth.*

Elevate USA is the national resources organization that works with new affil-iate cities to replicate Colorado UpLift (www.coloradouplift.org), expanding its proven program model, which has changed the lifetime trajectory of thousands of youths from Denver's low-income communities. These youths have completed high school and often college, developed strong families, and become community leaders. Others have gone on to become productive citizens through vocational training/certification or service careers such as the military.

This successful program has been replicated in five locations across the country Orlando, Phoenix, New York City, Indianapolis, and New England (Boston). St. Louis, Los Angeles, Detroit, and Las Vegas are other cities seriously considering the implementation the program.

Organization History and Description

Elevate USA emerged from the work of Colorado UpLift, a nonprofit youth services organization founded in Denver in 1982 with a mission of "Building Long-Term, Life-Changing Relationships with Urban Youth." The organizational model, a proven best practices program, has been teaching thirteen character qualities and life skills in the public schools, while providing a relationally driven mentoring program outside school over the past thirty-four years to urban youths. This holistic 24/7/365 relational approach has successfully decreased the high school dropout rate and increased the rate of enrollment into college, military, or technical training programs.

Each of the expansion cities mentioned above have results like Colorado UpLift, confirming the assumption that the program is replicable in diverse cities and communities. Colorado UpLift currently serves approximately 5,200 students annually, while the other five combined affiliates served approximately 3,000 students, indicating the potential for high impact and scope.

This replication success led Colorado UpLift to develop the Elevate USA organization, specifically dedicated to the purpose of launching new Elevate model programs, while strengthening the existing affiliate programs, ensuring best practices models throughout all affiliates.

Statement of Need

The foundational need—the development of successful urban youths who graduate from high school and go on to postsecondary training (college, vocational training/certification, or service career such as military)—is the reason Colorado UpLift, Elevate USA and its affiliate programs in Orlando, Phoenix, New York City, Indianapolis, and New England (Boston) exist. The average graduation rate for these urban schools across the United States rests around the 60 percent mark, whereas students who participate in the Elevate model collectively graduate over 90 percent.

Every year over 1.2 million students drop out of high school in the United States. Each year's class of dropouts will cost the country over $200 million during their lifetime in lost earnings and unrealized tax revenue. This monetary loss only shadows the greater social loss—that of precious lives of urban young people who have the potential of leading their communities into hope and prosperity.

Population Served

Elevate is dedicated to working with students in the most challenging urban communities across our country. They provide a "pipeline" of services with low-income students from fourth through twelfth grades, as well as providing support for alumni as they engage in college and other postsecondary training. All schools must have a high rate of 85+ percent reduced or free lunch to qualify for the program as well as high dropout rates, ensuring the organization is working for the communities of greatest need.

Elevate programs in Denver, Orlando, Phoenix, New York City, Indianapolis, and New England (Boston) are successfully providing a solution to this crisis in our low-income urban communities, radically changing the life trajectory of low-income youth in each city.

Program description: Elevate programs use a unique, relationship-based approach where full-time staff serve as teacher/mentors and life coaches, building relationships with students, available in their lives 24/7/365. These relationships are developed through four program components.

Four Program Components

In School—full-time teacher/mentors, representative of the communities served, teach accredited, elective high school classes in the public schools. These classes incorporate thirteen vital character qualities and life skills designed to develop the personal character, leadership abilities, and capabilities needed for success. The thirteen character qualities and life skills include vision, respect, caring, courage, responsibility, positive work ethic, integrity, career-mindedness, communication, leadership, problem solving, decision-making, and goal setting.

The high school students, having learned these lessons, teach fourth-grade students once weekly a hybrid class of the same lessons they learn five days weekly. This cross-age mentoring cements the lessons in the hearts and minds of the high school students while increasing a sense of accountability and leadership in their lives. Elevate teacher/mentors also teach seventh and eighth graders once weekly tailored to their learning level.

After-School Mentoring—it is the heart of the program, and it is where much of the life change occurs. One half of teachers/mentors' time is spent mentoring students after school, on weekends, and throughout the summer. The teachers/mentors pay attention to all children, discovering their talents, interests, and hope for the future by investing in their lives through activities and time together. Through these positive, caring relationships with nonparent adults, students begin to care and invest in their own futures.

Summer Adventure Programs—these provide growth through challenge and development of resiliency, leadership, and teamwork skills. Students participate in year-round outdoor activities, summer camps, team-building clinics, high-adventure activities, outdoor education, sports, and fitness activities.

Postsecondary Programs—through after-school workshops, in-class lessons, and one-on-one and group mentoring, students are encouraged to explore college options, instructed in the application process, directed toward scholarship opportunities, and given information necessary to persist in college. Some students interested in vocational training/certification also follow a similar process, while other students interested in a service career such as the military are directed to resources to pursue a positive future.

The success of Elevate rests on Four Program Distinctives running through all four of the components. These include:

Privately funded, salaried full-time teachers/mentors who often times have similar backgrounds to the youth they mentor. They understand the challenges faced by the young people they teach and mentor, giving them natural empathy and credibility. (Editor's note: The salaries are paid from Elevate funds so this is not a use of public funds.)

Long-term, 24/7/365 relational approach—Elevate provides a long-term pipeline of influence that follows students from fourth grade through high school graduation and beyond through formulation of "alumni" clubs. It is not limited to the school year. Students and teacher-mentors continue to build their relationships throughout the summer and school breaks.

Cross-age mentoring—High school students are equipped and given the opportunity to mentor elementary school students. These high school students step up as role models, become leaders and see firsthand the positive impact they can have on those around them.

Four program areas—The four different program areas—in school, after-school, summer/adventure, and postsecondary—make holistic mentoring possible.

Significant Program Outcomes

Elevate programs in the four initial cities Denver, Orlando, Phoenix, and New York have had consistent outcomes, including the following:

- Increase in graduation rates from an average of 58 percent to 90 percent for students who have participated for three or more years.
- 86 percent of Elevate students enroll in postsecondary training (college, vocational training/certification, or service career such as military).
- Demonstrated youth service and leadership in the community, including cross-age mentoring, summer camp internships, and community service activities such as traveling to Mexico to build houses for low-income residents.
- Growth in all thirteen character qualities/life skills areas. A six-year longitudinal study conducted by a third-party evaluator, included Colorado UpLift and selected affiliate programs, shows significant growth in all thirteen character qualities and life skills areas.

Summary

Elevate USA has a unique opportunity to positively affect change in our urban centers across the United States. Given the strong and effective history of Colorado UpLift and the successful replication demonstrated, Elevate USA has the foundation for significant influence and life-changing influence for tens of thousands of youths in multiple cities throughout our country, equipping urban youths for successful educational outcomes and productive lives.

THE OAKS ACADEMY

The Oaks Academy is located in Indianapolis, Indiana, at 2301 N. Park Street, 46250. The Oaks has grown from 53 students to 732 (2016) for their pre-K to grade 8 classes. The Oaks addresses the need for a quality, faith-based education downtown; it opened in 1998.

The students wear uniforms. There is an insistence that a "caring adult" supports the students; it is likely a parent but it does not have to be. This adult must show up at the school at least three times before pre-K admission. This requirement has some self-selection built into it that many of our *disruptive* students will not have a parent capable of making these visits. Nonetheless one half of these children come from a difficult background, and they are to be praised for their accomplishments.

Here is the school's mission statement:

*The Oaks Academy is a Christ-centered school that exists to provide a rich, clas-
sical education to children of diverse racial and socioeconomic backgrounds,
preparing them to succeed in a rigorous secondary educational program and to
demonstrate spiritual, social and emotional maturity.*

The Oaks Academy exists as a Christ-centered school, one that builds
strong moral character and spiritual depth in children, allowing them to dis-
cern their faith journeys as they grow in maturity. There is no faith requirement to be a student at The Oaks Academy, and they do not take a stance
on social issues. Nevertheless, the spiritual formation of children is important and is at work through an appropriate partnership between parents, the
school, and the family's place of worship.

The Oaks curriculum is based on a classical philosophy of education,
guided by a historic timeline that integrates all subjects and emphasizes deep
experience in the fine arts, science, math, and humanities to enhance learning
inside and outside of our school walls.

The Academy's claim to fame is that it consistently scores in the top 5 percent of the state in the ISTEP assessment exam and 95 percent of students
pass both the math and the English/language arts sections. Their most recent
accomplishment was the top score in the state on the 2014–2015 ISTEP
exam—the exam that was thrown out because it was so long and difficult.
More importantly, their students are developing a love for learning.

Mitch Daniels, former Indiana governor and current president of Purdue
University, was one of the founders of this school. He says:

Of all the things life has brought, this project is the most important human
endeavor I've been privileged to be a part of.

The Oaks Academy Habits:

The necessity of forming habits is an integral part of [our] philosophy as
they aid one in functioning in relationships. These are not tacked onto one's
life as another feat to be mastered in a performance culture, but are used
as valuable tools in the intellectual, spiritual, and physical development in
relationship to oneself, God, and others. Maryellen St. Cyr, *When Children
Love to Learn*

The habits are listed in the order that they are added at the grade levels.
All of these habits are promoted throughout the school at all grade levels, but
certain habits are a focus at each grade level. The habits are cumulative, and
middle school students are responsible for all of the habits on the list.

Beginning in Pre-K

Habit of attention: The habit of attention requires that one fix mind/body steadily on the matter at hand.

Habit of obedience: Obedience is demonstrated by responding immediately and completely to authority, as well as accepting consequences willingly.

Habit of respect: Showing respect involves using good manners and self-control in words and actions.

Habit of responsibility: Responsibility is shown when care is given to personal belongings and school property, and tasks are completed.

Added in Second Grade

Habit of reverence: Reverence is demonstrated by one's awe and respect for things of God.

Habit of reflection: The habit of reflection requires purposeful thinking and contemplation about the matter at hand.

Habit of thoroughness: Thoroughness involves completing whatever task is at hand to the very best of one's ability, leaving nothing undone.

Habit of punctuality: To be punctual, one's obligations must be met in a timely manner.

Added in Middle School

Habit of service: In serving, one must think of helping others and meeting their needs in a cheerful manner.

Habit of self-control: To be self-controlled is to have mastery over one's actions and have the ability to delay gratification.

Habit of integrity: Integrity involves always being honest and allowing one's words and actions to be above reproach, so that one is seen as trustworthy.

How the Academy Creates Hope

Recall that in chapter 4, the conceptual "Picture of Hope" was introduced. When this idea was discussed with Nathan Hand, director of advancement, he sketched out a profile that looks like the one in figure 5.3 (the dotted line is the line for their students).

There is no decline in the hope curve. He attributes this to the fact that they receive their students at the pre-K level, and they intervene so effectively the curve never drops.

Tables 5.1 and 5.2 show the nature of student body:

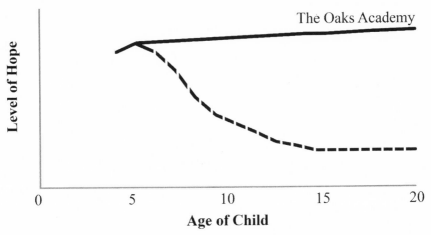

Figure 5.3.   The picture of hope for the Oaks Academy.

Table 5.2   The Oaks Academy Ethnicity of Student Body

African American	40%
White American	40%
Other American	20%

Table 5.3   The Oaks Academy of Socioeconomic Status

Low income	50%
Middle income	25%
High income	25%

Annual tuition costs for 2016–2017 school year:

Half day for pre-K and kindergarten: $8,400
Full day for pre-K and kindergarten: $9,890
Grades 1–5: $9,890
Grades 6–8: $10,110

Eighty-five percent of the students receive financial aid.
Interesting tidbits:

- Only about 1 percent of the students leave the school somewhere in their 10-year journey; this means the children stay in this program for years. Many public schools suffer from high turnover.
- There have only a few dismissals for disciplinary reasons in the history of the school.

> **TEXT BOX 5.4**
>
> There have only been a few dismissals for disciplinary reasons in the history of the school.

- They receive about forty applications for every available teaching position.
- Teaching salaries are competitive, and retention is very good.
- On the chart of Teacher's Emotional Bank Account introduced in chapter 4, they believe their teachers are near the top—I am changing lives/I love this job.
- Class size ranges from sixteen to eighteen students.
- Students are picked on a "first come first selected basis."
- School has ninety faculty and thirty-three nonfaculty.

Results:

After leaving the academy, their students attend some of the best high schools in the area. Their graduation rate from these schools is 99 percent.
Ninety-two percent of their students graduate from college.

SHEPHERD COMMUNITY CENTER[22]

The Shepherd Community is located at 4107 E. Washington St., Indianapolis, Indiana 46201. This area is a low-income part of Indianapolis. Their work goes well beyond simply working with children; they work with the entire community. A by-product is their educational impact on children, as will be articulated below.

Shepherd community is a faith-based, nonprofit organization established in 1985 with a straightforward sounding but staggering goal: to break the cycle of poverty on the near Eastside of Indianapolis. It seeks to do so by engaging and empowering the community to cultivate healthy children, strong families, and vibrant neighborhoods through a holistic programmatic approach that meets the physical, emotional, spiritual, and academic needs of its neighbors.

Addressing the Root Causes of Poverty

Shepherd's principal focus is on providing holistic, relational, social services to *children, youth, and families*. Yet it recognizes that the community environment in which its participating families live also matters greatly for their prospects for thriving. Shepherd participates in strategic partnerships aimed at such *neighborhood-level* improvements as quality housing, strong schools, crime reduction, and business and economic development.

The Essential Nature of Shepherd's Work

A Holistic Focus

Shepherd is committed to interventions of four basic types: physical, emotional, academic, and spiritual. Shepherd's aspiration is that this fourfold commitment is *infused* throughout the nonprofit's program design and implementation. Shepherd believes that only this *holistic* approach can nurture positive transformation in individuals and families.

Shepherd is not directly engaged in such important activities as affordable housing construction or business/economic development.

Eight Key Outcome Arenas

Through its fourfold holistic programming framed by the Continuum of Care and through its strategic partnerships, Shepherd directs its efforts toward transformation in eight key outcome arenas. Shepherd's Theory of Change posits that, taken together, an individual's or family's progress in these eight arenas can break the cycle of poverty. The eight outcome arenas are:

- Spiritual transformation among participants
- Empowerment of parents
- Educational success among youth
- Holistic health among youth and families
- Life skills growth among youth
- Increased positive adult relationships for youth
- Greater socioeconomic stability of families
- A stronger neighborhood

Results

The results for the Shepherd Center are less spectacular than The Oaks Academy and Elevate USA because they do not have a presence in the school system beyond the fifth grade. They do have their own school called the Shepherd Academy that enrolls children in pre-K to fifth grade. Table 5.4 shows graduation rates from several Indianapolis high schools located in the area served by the Shepherd Community Center.

The data shows the Shepherd Center students (who participate in their weekly and summer programs) have a high school graduation rate of 84 percent, and this rate is 22 percent higher than children who do not participate in Shepherd's programs. This is very impressive because the students are not a "captive audience" within a school. They voluntarily attend after-school programs and summer programs. Many of their programs have a heavy academic content so this is an aid to their buildup of competency.

For some time, the Shepherd Community Center ran an unaccredited pre-K to fifth-grade elementary school. In May of 2012, the pre-K to fifth-grade portion of the school was brought under the administration of Horizon Christian School and is treated as a second site for that school. They have assumed the educational administrative duties for the school thereby allowing Shepherd to continue to focus on its overall mission.

Table 5.5 shows some 2012 results for this school compared with the average of six Indianapolis Public Schools located in Shepherd's area.

As can be seen from table 5.5, the students at the Shepherd Academy do quite well when compared to the local public schools.

There are more positive results but the main point of this case study is the very positive outcomes for children when the impact is not directly in the classroom (all children above fifth grade) but in the after-school and summer programs of the center.

Table 5.4.   Comparing High School Graduation Rates—Shepherd Center

School	T.C. Howell HS	Emmerich Manual HS	Arsenal Technical HS	Irvington Community HS	Average for These Schools	Shepherd Community Participants[i]
High school graduation rate (%)	61	71	68	76	69	84

[i]Dr. Amy Sherman is the person who compiled these results. She estimates that there were 111 students that made up the 84 percent result. She cautions that their data has many weaknesses so the results must be interpreted carefully.

Table 5.5.   Shepherd Elementary School 2014 Academic Performance

Assessment	Shepherd Academy	Average of Six Indianapolis Public Elementary Schools	Shepherd's Percentage above Public Schools
I-Read 3 (% of total students passing)	87	62.5	39
ISTEP[i] (% of total students passing both parts)	64	48	33

[i]The ISTEP exam is Indiana's statewide assessment exam, formally titled Indiana Statewide Testing for Educational Progress. The state has decided to phase out this exam because of a number of issues, and they are currently looking for a replacement test.

FREEDOM WRITERS

This film is an excellent example of turning a classroom into a family. It illustrates some of the techniques teacher Erin Gruwell utilized to mold the tough high school students into a group of friends and trusted colleagues. She tried many traditional methods, and they failed but when she began to get the students talking about their lives, she better understood them as people, and they bonded together because of their similar backgrounds.

Freedom Writers is a 2007 drama film starring Hilary Swank, Scott Glenn, Imelda Staunton, and Patrick Dempsey. It is based on the book *The Freedom Writers Diary* by teacher Erin Gruwell who wrote the story based on Woodrow Wilson Classical High School in the Eastside neighborhood of Long Beach, California. The movie is also based on the District of Columbia program called City at Peace. The title is a play on the term "Freedom Riders," referring to the multiracial civil rights activists who tested the U.S. Supreme Court decision ordering the desegregation of interstate buses in 1961.

The idea for the film came from journalist Tracey Durning, who made a documentary about Erin Gruwell for the ABC News program Primetime Live. Durning served as coexecutive producer of the film. The film was dedicated to the memory of Armand Jones, who was killed after wrapping up Freedom Writers. He was eighteen and was shot to death in Anaheim, California, after a confrontation with a man who robbed Jones of a necklace in a Denny's restaurant.

To receive the full value of this program, you will need to acquire the film and watch the movie. We do not have statistics showing the longer-term success of this group of students.

ST. BENEDICTINES PREP SCHOOL, NEWARK, NEW JERSEY[23]

On June 26, 2016, the CBS television show *60 Minutes* featured a story on this most unusual school. The school is in the same spot in Newark, New Jersey, that it has held since 1868 and has seen many changes to its neighborhood yet they have prevailed and still actively educate students. This is another great example of changing the classroom into a family.

Note that there is an endnote associated with this section's title. This note gives the web addresses for three videos that explain this outstanding school. As can be seen in the YouTube clips, this school is quite unusual. To some degree, the students run the school. Discipline is not an issue as student leaders call morning convocation to order—all they do is raise one finger and the group of over 500 students comes to order.

One unique activity occurs at the conclusion of the spring session. The freshmen students are required to go on a five-day, fifty-three-mile hike/ camping trip on a section of the Appalachian Train that runs through New Jersey. For most students, this is a major ordeal, they carry their food, water, and tents. The upper-class leaders as well as their fellow students encourage them. This is a great way to teach grit, which must always be taught indirectly as opposed to head on.

Ninety-eight percent of their students graduate from this high school and 85 percent graduate from a university.

School Success

These five programs are a few examples of things that work; research will produce many more successful programs that are helping low-income children.

Paul Tough's new book titled *Helping Children Succeed*[24] focuses on the kind of situations we're covering here. Quoting from page 73 of his book:

> When kids feel a sense of belonging at school, when they receive the right kind of messages from an adult who believes they can succeed and who is attending to them with some degree of compassion and respect, they are more likely to show up to class, to persevere longer at difficult tasks, and to deal more resiliently with the countless small-scale setbacks and frustrations that make up a typical student's school day.
>
> In the same way that responsive parenting in early childhood creates a kind of mental space where a child's first tentative steps toward intellectual learning can take place, so do the right kind of messages from teachers in school create a mental space that allows a student to engage in more advanced and demanding academic learning.

The examples covered here truly set the higher-level expectations for the students and, through carefully developed methods, convince the students that they can manage their behavior and achieve academically.

Comments on This Book

This would be a great time to lay this research study next to a couple of other similar efforts to see how the numbers compare. As was mentioned earlier, this study is unique; at this point, this is a statement difficult to definitively prove but intense study is unable to find anything even close. At one point, an educational expert was engaged and she too says she has never seen such a study. So, we have nothing that is comparable for side-by-side review.

As an outsider, it is a surprise that school administrators, schools of education, and others have not tried to assess and publish the impact of unruly students on the learning environment. This lack of knowledge is a major impediment to the completion of their mission to educate all children. For the school targeted for this study apparently, they had no idea that so much time in each class was being wasted. Of course, there are other grades in the school, and they too are wasting a lot of time in classroom management. Our targeted four fourth grades are only the tip of the iceberg.

The explanation of why there is no quantified knowledge of disruptive children has already been covered in this book. Schools of education, in particular, probably think, "If they would just teach the way we taught them, they would not have classroom management issues." A retired Indiana University School of Education professor read the original paper and commented: "It sounds like a bunch of whining to me."

It is known from the 2004 study by Public Agenda that 85 percent of the teachers and 73 percent of the parents in their study acknowledge that the school experience of most students suffers at the expense of a few chronic offenders. The Public Agenda study says a small number of children disturb the learning of the others. In our case study, 23 percent is *not* a small number.

No generalizations are safe about the loss of instructional time in other schools in the state or the nation because to do so would not be accurate. Some probably have similar issues and others do not. In fact, the list of 114 Indiana schools graded A given in chapter 4 are all high-poverty neighborhoods, and they probably do not experience much lost instructional time.

Always remember that the issues discussed in this book are socioeconomic and not racial. Communities where parents have great difficulty in earning a living or for some other reason they are unable to be effective parents will often produce *disruptive* children.

After the original paper was completed (see appendix C), it was read or discussed with approximately thirty teachers and other educators—their most frequent response was, "You're spot on, that's the way it is." No one rejected the proposition that a group of difficult-to-manage students can almost destroy a classroom (and the teacher at the same time).

One of the reviewing teachers was a retired kindergarten teacher from Racine, Wisconsin—she said the paper described her kindergarten class. One of her *disruptive* students bashed the head of another student on a urinal, and the young man needed stitches. One reviewer was a highly respected retired principal in an Indianapolis township school system. He felt our estimate of sixty-two minutes of lost time/day/classroom was too low. In other words, it's worse than we portrayed. Another couple of reviewers were not as explicit but they too felt the time loss was too low.

Chapter 6

Dramatic Improvements Are Needed

REVIEW—TAKEAWAYS

This book makes many points and observations. Here is a selection of some of the more important material with a reference as to where more information can be found within this book.

Figures 2.2 and 2.3 were given in chapter 2. These graphs should shock us all. It says students' competence in math and reading has remained essentially flat for forty-one years! (page 6)

The teaching profession in the United States is suffering from many negative influences. Some of the issues are summarized below as the evidence:

1. Low teacher morale
2. Poor teacher retention
3. Enrollment in many of the countries' schools of education is dropping—this will lead to a teacher shortage
4. Low teacher status

TEXT BOX 2.1

A teacher shortage is just the beginning of a huge workforce development problem if not corrected. (page 13)

Do teachers have autonomy? Absolutely not, their profession is one of the most unempowered professions in America.

TEXT BOX 2.4

A businessman views a bureaucracy as overhead; a bureaucrat sees it as power. The more people managed, the more money made. (page 22)

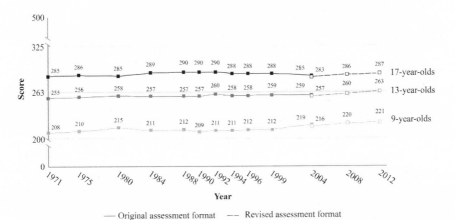

Figure 2.2. **Average reading-scale scores on the long-term trend National Assessment of Education Progress (NAEP), by age: selected years 1971–2012. (page 7)**

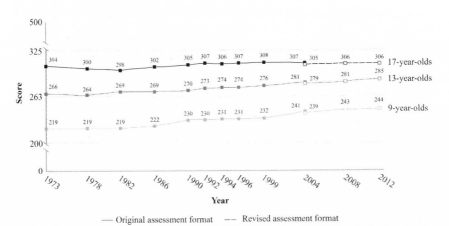

Figure 2.3. **Average mathematics-scale scores on the long-term trend National Assessment of Education Progress (NAEP), by age: selected years 1973–2012. (page 7)**

Text Box 3.1 contains some experienced advice from a minister who heads up the Shepherd Community Center on the east side of Indianapolis:

TEXT BOX 3.1

Programs don't work, people do. Relationship with caring adults is essential for success. (page 28)

For young fourth graders, it is essential that they possess character and grit not just to produce success when they are thirty years old but so that they can be successful in class tomorrow, the day after, and so on. (page 33)

OTHER MEMORABLE THOUGHTS

Grit can substitute for intellect. Intellect cannot be a substitute for grit. (page 33)

In our judgment, our students, with some exceptions, have the native intellectual capacity to pass the ISTEP exam or do well on any assessment test. At the current time, there are barriers that get in the way of their ability to grow and apply these skills in an effective way—these barriers will be discussed below. (page 44)

This book will emphasize several times that it is a child behavior of a group of children that is at issue, not their mental capacity. (page 44)

If someone tells you a school is in the 70–100 percent free and reduced meal percentages, there is only a 29 percent chance that it is a D- or F-graded school. This is a very significant conclusion. (page 44)

It is not allowed for one student to interfere in the education of another. (page 67)

The teachers were not upset about teaching; they were upset because of their inability to teach. (page 41)

It was apparent with this group that though the higher administration often speaks for the teachers, it seldom speaks to them. (page 41)

Figure 3.4. Success equation (page 32).

Table 4.6.   Calculation of Average School Type Grade Point Average (page 50)

School Type	Avg. GPA 2013	Avg. GPA 2014	New Data! Avg. GPA 2016	Number of Schools
Traditional public	2.9	3.1	2.6	1,758
Religious/independent	3.2	3.4	3.0	279
Charter schools	1.5	1.6	1.7	58

Table 4.6 illustrates the poor performance of charter schools in Indiana. They get graded a D+, while the other schools are much higher.

What doesn't work (page 75)

"The results from our incentive experiments on student achievement are surprising." "The impact of financial incentives on student achievement is statistically 0 in each city."

"I find no evidence that teacher incentives increase student performance, attendance or graduation; nor do I find evidence that incentives change student or teacher behavior." "If anything, teacher incentives may decrease student achievement, especially in large schools."

The teachers created the below findings in the research facilitated at an Indianapolis area grade school:

1. Students in any classroom can be divided into three classifications; also shown here is the average percentage occurrence in the four fourth grades studied: (page 56)

    a. The *engaged* student—31 percent
    b. The *follower* students—46 percent
    c. The *disruptive* students—23 percent

2. Data reveals that each day, in every classroom, sixty-two minutes is lost in classroom management issues, primarily driven by the *disruptive* students. A breakdown of the sixty-two minutes reveals that each teacher will face forty-six minutes of disciplinary issues each and every day. (page 66)
3. When analyzing why the *disruptive* students were not able to successfully deal with the classroom situation, we discovered they lack character and grit. (page 68)
4. The teachers were led through a root cause analysis to uncover why the students lack the necessary skills. Here are the root causes: (page 69)

    a. Parents/parenting

b. Culture

c. By choice

5. The *disruptive* students need to be moved to a separate classroom—they must take a more suitable educational journey. (page 81)

TEXT BOX 4.8

It is terribly wrong for this group of disruptive students to deprive the balance of the class, students who are amenable to education, from an opportunity to learn and excel. (page 60)

Students who are lacking in certain parenting influence (*disruptives*) need to be placed in a classroom that does six things: (page 82)

1. Emphasizes/teaches character and grit
2. Utilizes discipline as a teaching tool
3. Values are taught and ingrained into all students
4. Provides an environment of fellowship and camaraderie—something they are missing at home
5. Has a substantial amount of caring adult intervention
6. Continues to teach the required course material

TEXT BOX 5.2

Turn the classroom into a family. (page 85)

Opinion: The only children that should be receiving government-funded pre-K schooling are children like our *disruptive* students. Recall that these children are very difficult to manage who receive very little support from their parents; in fact shortfalls in parenting is a root cause for their behavioral problems in the classroom. Any training they receive should be rich in noncognitive skills along with cognitive. These students need self-control so that they can be good classroom students later in their journey—they need character and grit! (page 87)

CONCLUSIONS AND ACTION STEPS

On November 7, 1962, Richard Nixon had his last news conference. One of his most famous declarations was made in that meeting. He says to the press: "You're going to miss me when I'm gone; you don't have Nixon to kick around anymore, because, gentlemen, this is my last press conference."

This quotation comes to mind because teachers are a bit like Nixon. Unless the U.S. school administrators, politicians, citizens, and others start treating teachers with more respect, we're no longer going to have teachers to "kick around." Many of them are going to be doing something else. There is a major shortage of teachers on the immediate horizon, and there are no signs that it is going to get better.

In chapter 2, it was observed that the national reading and math assessment scores have been flat for forty-one years. It was pointed out that during the last many years, the governments have added layer upon layer of laws and bureaucracies at the national level, state levels, and district levels, yet there has been no improvement. It is reasonable to conclude that these laws and bureaucratic organizations did no good and in fact could well be part of the problem. It is also reasonable to conclude that poor performance like the reading and math scores had to be the result of a major systemic problem.

Two (of several possible) sources to blame for a systemic problem are teachers and/or students. It is difficult to fathom how almost all the public-school teachers in America could be blamed for these results. On the other hand, students themselves are never discussed as a source of the trouble and for their possible involvement in this national problem.

This book discusses student issues and how they impact the schools. The *disruptive* students (really, the parents) deserve a significant level of blame for contributing to this national education problem.

The teachers involved either directly or indirectly with this book say the students have the intellectual capability to pass assessment exams. Recall from chapter 4, data is presented in an attempt to prove that the students have the needed mental skills. It's something else causing the problem; in this book, it is referred to as an absence of character and grit. Fortunately, it is only a small percentage of the students, but they have a big impact on their classmates who want to learn. These troublesome students are called the *disruptive* students. There is hope; these students can change and they can be taught the missing skills; chapter 5 gives examples of schools that have been successful in this pursuit.

The problem of *disruptive* students plays an important negative role in many of the problems in U.S. public education. Here are some of the areas impacted:

1. Poor student performance
2. Poor student morale

3. Poor teacher morale
4. Low teacher status
5. High teacher turnover
6. Large drop-offs in students wanting to become teachers leading to a shortage of trained teachers
7. Poor public perception of the U.S. education system
8. Unjustified criticism of teachers
9. Disruptive students in our classrooms waste significant amounts of time thereby interfering with the education of the students in the class who want to learn
10. School discipline is generally lacking in many schools so the *disruptive* students do not face consequences
11. Violence against teachers

Why Blame Students (Parents)?

The Public Agenda study, *Teaching Interrupted, Do Discipline Policies in Today's Public Schools Foster the Common Good?*, establishes that the U.S. public and teachers are well aware of many of the problems facing our public schools. Their results show that a few persistent problem students are negatively impacting the school experience of the balance of the classes. This report also finds that discipline is needed and wanted by both parents and teachers. This study, because of its national opinion sampling, makes the issue of student behavior and lack of school discipline a national problem. The absence of discipline is a management problem—not a problem to be blamed on the children. Unfortunately, human nature and behavior can naturally trend to disarray when folks are put together in groups. It is leadership that brings order to chaos; it usually will not happen on its own.

The school research covered in this book confirms that there are students, called *disruptive students*, who, either directly or indirectly, cause 28 percent of the class's instructional time to be wasted. The *Teaching Interrupted* study was survey based and made no attempt to quantify the number of persistent problem students other than to say it is a small group of students. The research reported in this report quantifies the number of persistent problem students at 23 percent—a lot more than "a few or a small group."

Why is nothing heard from the educational community about these persistent *disruptive students*? Educators will not blame students or parents for any of their problems; that is a short path to job termination. After two presentations of the material in this book and numerous reviews of the original paper, active or recently retired educators say this material is "spot on," but they cannot admit it in public.

Since there is no outcry from the educational community, the general public must assume that "they have the problem under control" when in fact it is not even close to being controlled.

So Much for Incentive Pay—It Does Not Work

Two very large experiments aimed at motivating teachers and students with monetary rewards for improvements in performance resulted in zero performance increases thus pointing out the money is not the issue; intrinsic motivation is the issue, motivation that comes from within the teacher or the student. A key motivating element for a teacher is empowerment (provides autonomy, one of the three needs developed by Deci and Ryan).

Teachers must be changing lives to truly be motivated; this will position them in the positive portion of their emotional bank account. Children, on the other hand, can be motivated by competence—the very act of learning can be a very self-satisfying and motivating force. Many children face negative external forces so they are going to be a more difficult challenge but success with these children is being accomplished across our nation.

School Administrations Are Not Helping Teacher Morale

As a businessperson, it is objectionable that the politicians and school administrators are placing many of their teachers into these almost impossible situations. They say good luck; have a great year. Generally, when a business puts someone in a position, he or she has proper training and a *good support system* to help make him or her successful. In the case of teachers, dismissing students from class, taking them to the office, forbidding recess, and so on is viewed as a teacher failure, not as a necessary disciplinary control step.

As has been demonstrated in this book, much of the blame should be placed on the misbehaving students and their parenting. The teachers cannot be absolved of responsibility, but it is for sure that they are not solely to blame.

It will be necessary to restructure the classrooms, by moving all the *disruptive* students to a single class, simply to provide the other students with teachers who have the needed skills to teach. This is not to say that these teachers are not competent, but that managing the *disruptive* students requires a different curriculum and special teaching/classroom management skills. If something isn't done to restore discipline, there are going to be many, many openings for teachers.

Empower and Elevate Teachers

It would seem that everyone but the teachers are involved in the "what do we do to get better" dialogue. Teachers are the most unempowered profession in the United States. Control has been moved further and further away from the local communities and from the teachers. This gets back to the Total Quality process used to facilitate the school research project. The first step in the four-step scheme is: if you want to understand and improve a job, *ask the people who do the job.*

Industry has made millions and millions of dollars employing this simple step. Not only do they get good ideas, they create autonomy, which is one of the three needs specified by Deci and Ryan as essential to motivate individuals.

Be aware that many of the good ideas that led to the creation of this book came from teachers. They were facilitated, but they were very easy to lead through the process, and they were "all in." This is not always the case as many folks "dig in their heels" and create barriers to team progress. There is so much more they can do if only they were empowered to help.

There Is Work for Caring Adults

In chapter 3, the vital importance of caring adults in the life of a child is an emphatic requirement. Children without hope cannot be successful. Having caring adults is one way to keep the level of hope high or to restore it if it has declined. Obviously, the best source of caring would be the parent/parents but this is not always a reality.

Here is where the public can help—get involved, join Big Brothers Big Sisters, service clubs can help, tutor children at school, join church groups that support schools, mentor children, and so on. Your work can make a dramatic difference in the life of a child in need. This is the only way we can break the multigenerational poverty in America.

How to Teach the Disruptive Students

Disruptive students are causing problems because of their behavior not because they lack the necessary intelligence. In the section Looking for Root Cause (chapter 4), the teachers enumerated some of the skills these students are lacking. This set of "missing attributes" is part of a set of skills called character and grit. As is pointed out, the "success equation" for a student is composed of two kinds of skills: (1) intellectual skills and (2) character and grit.

In past times these latter skills were imparted to children by their parent/parents, their church, other relatives, and so on but in today's world of the disintegration of the traditional family, some parents do not teach these skills to their children.

Fortunately, these missing skills are teachable, and more and more schools are working to include something like "Character and Leadership" into their programs. They realize that the success equation is a reality, and they need to add this kind of training to keep children in school and to make them better citizens. Reestablishing discipline is a great way to teach/reinforce good behavior, part of the by-product of character and grit.

The five "success" stories given in chapter 5 are examples of how these skills are taught. These are only five of many examples of successful approaches to teaching this type of students. If one reflects on what is going on in these schools, it is this:

TEXT BOX 6.7

They are turning the classroom into a family.

Action Steps

Here is a set of suggested action steps for school administrators that will help to alleviate the lost time issue of *disruptive* students:

1. Research and document a curriculum rich in the instruction of character and grit that will be used to teach the *disruptive* students once they have been removed from the regular classes.[1]
2. Develop a plan to establish a class for each grade (K–12) that will be made up of *disruptive* students. It is imperative to remove these students from the regular classrooms in order to allow the balance of the class to have effective instruction.
3. Make a commitment and develop and implement a plan to restore discipline to the school and to each classroom. It is proposed that discipline is actually taught as part of a course. This is a wonderful way to teach character and grit to all students.
4. Develop an advisory board made up of teachers who will assist in the management of the educational system at both the school and district levels. This action will begin the empowerment of teachers. Another panel of selected teachers can provide guidance to the state school board, the governor, and the legislature.
5. Give student awards to recognize academic excellence to students. The high school in Avon, Indiana gives letter sweaters of the same style and size as an academic letter. Raise academics above sports and band.
6. Go to lengths to boost teacher morale. Work hard to put them in the positive range of the teacher's emotional bank account.
7. If the risk of lawsuits is high because of these changes, the state should institute a "case review" step like the system used for malpractice lawsuits

here in Indiana. A panel of doctors reviews the cases and decides whether or not "good practice" was followed. If yes, there will be no trial; if no, a trial will follow. More than likely school administrators and teachers face many lawsuits that are "without merit"—cases that should be removed from the system. This review panel will remove some of the supposed "malpractice threats" from the system.

Most of All, Children's Education Must Be a Critical Issue

When a teacher does something controversial, or when the testing scores are released each year, the news lights up with controversy over education. Fingers are pointed; we talk about how one party or the other is ruining education, and then we go back to our other concerns. Popular but terrible movies are produced that glamorize school misconduct and make the teachers look idiotic.

At a high level, above individual schools and teachers, the problem is national apathy.

The reality is that the public does not realize how essential the educational system is to our future. The country does not show teachers the level of respect in society they deserve. There is a prevailing attitude, if you cannot do "something important," teach. This is what happens to people who cannot get a real job! After all, anyone can teach. Quite to the contrary, good teaching is difficult, tiring, and demanding. It is noble and important work that needs good talent to help tend the crop of children coming through the school systems. As long as education takes a backseat in our national priorities, it will always get our secondhand solutions as well.

There Is Hope

This book is full of hope. It has defined one of the big problems in education and shown a way schools have overcome the burdens of teaching children in poverty. The children can pass the assessment exams; they can be taught the needed skills and values. The role of hope and the importance of character and grit to a child's success are emphasized. This problem can be whipped, but the nation must rise out of our collective apathy and support teachers, politicians, and school systems to empower them to make the proper decisions and then implement the resulting programs.

Epilogue

Son John was one of the four teachers in the research project that is behind this book. It was John who called many days to relate some of the unbelievable events of bad behavior that were taking place in his and other classrooms. It was John that suggested how to break up the students in their classes into three groups:

The engaged students
The follower students
The disruptive students

Together with the other teachers, he crafted the very workable definitions for each student type. He was a major contributor all along the way as we completed our project.

After sixteen years as an elementary teacher, his emotional bank account hit bottom, and he resigned his position early in the 2015–2016 school year. This was not an easy choice because he loved his kids, and most of them loved him. However, with 23 percent of his class essentially unmanageable and with no real support from his administration, he realized the futility of continuing to teach. He took a major pay cut and moved to a job that was not ideal, but it did get him out of the classroom.

He was a teacher because he wanted to change lives and help the children reach their full potential. Unfortunately, the only thing that changed was John. It is humiliating to have some students treat their teachers with such disrespect and have no recourse. There were essentially no consequences for anything but the most extreme behavior. The parents of the *disruptive* students were a great frustration because dealing with them was generally a very negative experience. The principal was of no particular value when dealing with the children; she had very little impact on the *disruptive* children or their parents.

So, some teachers bite the dust and their story gets spread around, and others share their same frustrations—some of them will resign as well.

Last spring John went back to pay a visit to his teacher friends at his school and to see how they were doing. Not surprising most of the teachers were operating in the negative portion of their emotional bank account, and morale was low. He said he was not in a particularly good mood when he got to school; however, when he left, he was in a great mood because he knew, in spite of his difficult decision to leave education, it was the right call.

Appendix A

The Full List of 114 High-Poverty Schools Graded A

Table A.1 shows the list of all 114 high-poverty schools graded A.

Table A.1.   Full List of Indiana Hit Parade of Schools 2013–2014.

School District	School Name	County	Grade	Meal %
1 Peru Community Schools	Elmwood Primary Learning Center	Miami	A	70
2 Anderson Preparatory Academy	Anderson Preparatory Academy	Madison	A	70.1
3 Fort Wayne Community Schools	Waynedale Elementary School	Allen	A	70.3
4 Perry Township Schools	Southport 6th Grade Academy	Marion	A	70.3
5 Vigo County School Corp	Sugar Grove Elementary School	Vigo	A	70.5
6 Fayette County School Corp	Eastview Elementary School	Fayette	A	71
7 Fort Wayne Community Schools	Northwood Middle School	Allen	A	71
8 Fort Wayne Community Schools	Maplewood Elementary School	Allen	A	71.2
9 Crawford Co Com School Corp	Patoka Elementary School	Crawford	A	71.3
10 Greater Clark County Schools	Maple Elementary School	Clark	A	71.3
11 Goshen Community Schools	Waterford Elementary School	Elkhart	A	71.6
12 Bartholomew Con School Corp	Lillian Schmitt Elem School	Bartholomew	A	71.7

(Continued)

Table A.1. (Continued)

	School District	School Name	County	Grade	Meal %
13	Crawford Co Com School Corp	Marengo Elementary School	Crawford	A	71.9
14	North White School Corp	North White Primary School	White	A	71.9
15	Vincennes Community Sch Corp	Francis Vigo Elementary Sch	Knox	A	71.9
16	Lafayette School Corporation	Glen Acres Elementary School	Tippecanoe	A	72
17	DeKalb Co Ctl United Sch Dist	Waterloo Elementary School	Dekalb	A	72.2
18	Perry Township Schools	William Henry Burkhart Elem	Marion	A	72.4
19	Fort Wayne Community Schools	John S Irwin Elementary Sch	Allen	A	72.5
20	Clay Community Schools	East Side Elementary School	Clay	A	72.6
21	South Bend Community Sch Corp	Darden Primary Center	St. Joseph	A	72.7
22	School City of Hammond	Kenwood Elementary School	Lake	A	72.8
23	M S D Lawrence Township	Indian Creek Elem Sch	Marion	A	73.1
24	Scott County School District 1	Austin Middle School	Scott	A	73.1
25	Seymour Community Schools	Margaret R Brown Elem School	Jackson	A	73.1
26	Elkhart Community Schools	Osolo Elementary School	Elkhart	A	73.2
27	Fort Wayne Community Schools	Mabel K Holland Elem Sch	Allen	A	73.2
28	School City of Mishawaka	Liberty Elementary School	St. Joseph	A	73.3
29	Monroe County Com Sch Corp	Templeton Elementary School	Monroe	A	73.5
30	Beech Grove City Schools	South Grove Intermediate School	Marion	A	73.7
31	Randolph Eastern School Corp	North Side Elementary School	Randolph	A	73.7
32	Vincennes Community Sch Corp	James Whitcomb Riley Elem Sch	Knox	A	73.7
33	Fort Wayne Community Schools	Indian Village Elementary Sch	Allen	A	73.9
34	Indianapolis Public Schools	Cold Spring School	Marion	A	74.1
35	Michigan City Area Schools	Springfield Elementary School	LaPorte	A	74.4

	School District	School Name	County	Grade	Meal %
36	Vigo County School Corp	Terre Town Elementary School	Vigo	A	75
37	Greenwood Community Sch Corp	Greenwood Northeast Elem Sch	Johnson	A	75.1
38	Muncie Community Schools	North View Elementary School	Delaware	A	75.2
39	New Albany-Floyd Co Con Sch	Hazelwood Middle School	Floyd	A	75.2
40	East Noble School Corp	North Side Elementary School	Noble	A	75.6
41	LaPorte Community School Corp	Hailmann Elementary School	LaPorte	A	75.7
42	Fort Wayne Community Schools	Brentwood Elementary School	Allen	A	75.9
43	Evansville Vanderburgh Sch Corp	Tekoppel Elementary School	Vanderburgh	A	76.3
44	Marion Community Schools	Riverview Elementary School	Grant	A	76.4
45	Indianapolis Public Schools	Crispus Attucks Medical Magnet HS	Marion	A	76.9
46	Jay School Corp	Judge Haynes Elementary Sch	Jay	A	76.9
47	Greater Clark County Schools	Northaven Elementary School	Clark	A	77.1
48	Fort Wayne Community Schools	Franke Park Elementary School	Allen	A	77.2
49	M S D Warren Township	Creston Intermediate Academy	Marion	A	77.2
50	M S D Warren Township	Hawthorne Elementary School	Marion	A	77.3
51	Indianapolis Public Schools	Jonathan Jennings School 109	Marion	A	77.6
52	Fort Wayne Community Schools	Northcrest Elementary School	Allen	A	77.9
53	South Bend Community Sch Corp	Jefferson Intermediate Center	St Joseph	A	78
54	Fort Wayne Community Schools	Harrison Hill Elementary Sch	Allen	A	78.4
55	Lake Station Community Schools	Carl J Polk Elementary School	Lake	A	79.1
56	Lake Station Community Schools	Virgil I Bailey Elementary School	Lake	A	79.4
57	Michigan City Area Schools	Knapp Elementary School	LaPorte	A	79.4
58	Perry Township Schools	Homecroft Elementary School	Marion	A	79.4

(Continued)

Table A.1. (Continued)

School District	School Name	County	Grade	Meal %
59 School Town of Speedway	James A Allison Elem School 3	Marion	A	80
60 M S D Lawrence Township	Sunnyside Elementary Sch	Marion	A	80.1
61 M S D Pike Township	Deer Run Elementary	Marion	A	80.1
62 M S D Pike Township	Central Elementary School	Marion	A	80.3
63 River Forest Community Sch Corp	John I Meister Elementary School	Lake	A	80.6
64 Indianapolis Public Schools	Ernie Pyle School 90	Marion	A	80.8
65 Indianapolis Public Schools	Francis W Parker School 56	Marion	A	81
66 Anderson Community School Corp	Edgewood Elementary School	Madison	A	81.7
67 Perry Township Schools	Southport Elementary School	Marion	A	81.8
68 Lafayette School Corporation	Vinton Elementary School	Tippecanoe	A	82.2
69 Clay Community Schools	Forest Park Elementary School	Clay	A	83
70 Lafayette School Corporation	Miami Elementary School	Tippecanoe	A	83
71 Vigo County School Corp	Blanche E Fuqua Elem Sch	Vigo	A	83
72 Elkhart Community Schools	Monger Elementary School	Elkhart	A	83.5
73 M S D Wayne Township	McClelland Elementary School	Marion	A	84.2
74 Michigan City Area Schools	Lake Hills Elementary School	LaPorte	A	84.3
75 River Forest Community Sch Corp	River Forest Intermediate	Lake	A	84.5
76 M S D Wayne Township	Chapel Glen Elementary School	Marion	A	84.6
77 M S D Wayne Township	Chapelwood Elementary School	Marion	A	84.9
78 Richmond Community Schools	Fairview Elementary School	Wayne	A	85.1
79 Lafayette School Corporation	Murdock Elementary School	Tippecanoe	A	85.7
80 Anderson Community School Corp	Valley Grove Elementary Sch	Madison	A	86.2
81 M S D Washington Township	Greenbriar Elementary School	Marion	A	86.3
82 New Albany-Floyd Co Con Sch	Fairmont Elementary School	Floyd	A	86.4

School District	School Name	County	Grade	Meal %
83 Vigo County School Corp	Farrington Grove Elem Sch	Vigo	A	86.4
84 Vigo County School Corp	West Vigo Elementary School	Vigo	A	86.5
85 River Forest Community Sch Corp	Henry S Evans Elementary Sch	Lake	A	87.2
86 Elkhart Community Schools	Hawthorne Elementary School	Elkhart	A	87.5
87 Anderson Community School Corp	Tenth Street Elementary Sch	Madison	A	88
88 Perry Township Schools	Clinton Young Elem Sch	Marion	A	88.1
89 Fort Wayne Community Schools	Washington Elem School	Allen	A	88.2
90 M S D Wayne Township	Maplewood Elementary School	Marion	A	88.8
91 Fort Wayne Community Schools	Fairfield Elementary School	Allen	A	89.3
92 Indianapolis Public Schools	Carl Wilde School 79	Marion	A	89.6
93 Indianapolis Public Schools	Arlington Woods Elementary School	Marion	A	89.7
94 Fort Wayne Community Schools	South Wayne Elementary School	Allen	A	90.8
95 School City of Hammond	Abraham Lincoln Elem Sch	Lake	A	90.9
96 Anderson Community School Corp	Erskine Elementary School	Madison	A	91
97 Lake Ridge Schools	Longfellow Elementary School	Lake	A	91.1
98 Fort Wayne Community Schools	Levan R Scott Academy	Allen	A	91.5
99 M S D Wayne Township	Garden City Elementary School	Marion	A	92
100 M S D Wayne Township	Rhoades Elementary School	Marion	A	92.2
101 Gary Community School Corp	Frankie W McCullough Acad for Girl	Lake	A	92.3
102 Evansville Vanderburgh Sch Corp	Evans School	Vanderburgh	A	92.9
103 Indianapolis Public Schools	Brookside School 54	Marion	A	93.1
104 Vigo County School Corp	Benjamin Franklin Elem School	Vigo	A	93.3
105 Muncie Community Schools	Longfellow Elementary School	Delaware	A	93.5

(Continued)

Table A.1. (Continued)

School District	School Name	County	Grade	Meal %
106 Gary Community School Corp	Daniel Hale Williams Elem Sch	Lake	A	93.7
107 School City of East Chicago	George Washington Elem School	Lake	A	94.2
108 School City of East Chicago	William McKinley Elementary Sch	Lake	A	94.2
109 M S D Wayne Township	Stout Field Elementary School	Marion	A	94.4
110 Anderson Community School Corp	Anderson Elementary School	Madison	A	96.4
111 School City of Hammond	Lafayette Elementary School	Lake	A	96.8
112 School City of East Chicago	Abraham Lincoln Elementary Sch	Lake	A	97.7
113 Evansville Vanderburgh Sch Corp	Delaware Elementary School	Vanderburgh	A	97.9
114 School City of East Chicago	Carrie Gosch Elementary School	Lake	A	98.3

Appendix B

The Original Paper: *What's It Like to Teach in a School Graded D?*

This white paper was published on the website: Failingschool.org in August 2014. This is the write-up of the work that is behind this book. It is presented for the reader who would like to know more about the how this research effort began. Note that there are some changes in terminology from that used in the book, for example, the different students were called: type 1, type 2, and type 3. These titles are no longer used.

WHAT'S IT LIKE TO TEACH IN A SCHOOL GRADED D?

Note to reader: We are four experienced fourth grade elementary teachers who, through this paper, are commenting on teaching in our elementary school. Our school is located in central Indiana and was recently given a "D" grade.

We are extremely disappointed, though not totally surprised, that our school was judged so harshly. We believe that the grading program for the state is unfair in considering test results so heavily in setting the school grade. We are not competing on a level playing field. In grading schools, some consideration must be given to socioeconomic conditions at the school. Below is our story.

Executive Summary

Recently the state of Indiana began the process of grading schools. Our school was given a grade of "D." We respond to this grade by conveying some of the hurdles we face on a daily basis. At the outset, we make the declaration that our students have, with a few exceptions, the intellectual skills to pass the ISTEP[1] exams or most any other type of basic skills evaluation scheme. The fact that our school was rated D illustrates that their actual performance is lacking—we address the causes for this lack of performance in this paper.

The students in each class are divided into three types:

1. The conscientious student
2. The follower
3. The problem student

Type 3 students exert a heavy influence over the type 2 and tend to pull them down. As a result of the large number of type 3 students, managing the class is very difficult and time consuming. Our analysis explains that in a typical classroom, sixty-two minutes of each day are lost to classroom management activities; sixty-two minutes is 27 percent loss of the available instruction time. Of this, 53 percent, or 37 minutes, can be attributed to the type 3 students. Breaking this down further reveals that twenty-four minutes of the thirty-seven minutes, 73 percent, is due to the conduct/attitude issues of the type 3 students. We also point out that the twenty-four minutes associated with the remaining students in the classroom (about 18 in number) could be dramatically reduced if the influence of the type 3 students could be eliminated. In the latter sections of this paper, we make suggestions as to how to lower the impact of the type 3 students.

Introduction

Every year when the ISTEP results are made public, the Indianapolis Star posts the results in their newspaper. People can see exactly which schools passed ISTEP and which schools failed. The schools and the students are reduced to numbers and percentages. What percentage of students passed over all? What will be our school's grade? We're entering a new world.

And now, with all the school reforms, this pass or fail status is crucial; it is crucial to the administrators and teachers. Our livelihoods depend on getting kids to pass the test. But what if you are in a school where many kids don't care about the test? There is a reason why certain districts consistently succeed and certain districts consistently fail, and it is not necessarily the quality of the teachers. While good teachers are extremely important, we would contend that good students and good parents are just as important if not more so.

Student quality and student motivation are the missing components in the public discussion on school quality. There are significant issues with the quality and motivation of some of the students. When we say quality of the students, we are not saying they are intellectually inferior but we are saying that they carry heavy burdens from their life outside of school that make it difficult for them to learn.

These burdens also make it particularly difficult for them to be taught. In addition, their social behavior makes it very challenging to establish a classroom-learning environment and as a result other students (and there are many), who want to learn, are impacted by their disruptive behavior. Over the years in almost any school, every teacher has had to deal with "unruly" students; in a D-rated school, there are so many problem-creating children that it impacts the entire school.

Some Characteristics of Our School

In addition to the concern about the quality and motivation of some of our students, our school experiences a total school turnover of approximately 25 percent each year. This means if you begin the year with twenty-five students in your class then by the end of the school year, about six of your students will "turnover." In other words, you'll lose six and gain new six students. Another indicator of the nature of a school is the extent to which the government subsidizes meals—83 percent of our students are on some type of lunch program. (Based on 2011–2012 numbers.) Only 51.2 percent of the fourth-grade students passed both the English/language arts and math exams during the 2012 testing round.[2]

Intellectual Capability

In our judgment, our students, with some exceptions, have the native intellectual capacity to pass the ISTEP exam or do well on any assessment test. At the current time, there are barriers that get in the way of their ability to grow and apply these skills in an effective way—these barriers will be discussed below.

Types of Students

Every classroom, no matter what school is considered, will have three types of students:

1. A type 1 students can be counted on to act with integrity the vast majority of the time. They are the ones who stay in their seat and keep working quietly if the teacher has to step out of the room. When their teacher is teaching, their eyes are either on the teacher, or on the material that the teacher is teaching from. Either way, they are actively listening and participating in the lesson. When given an assignment, they get busy immediately. They will sit at their desk, or in their assigned spot and work. They raise their hand if they have trouble. They never call out if they have a question. It is very rare that such type of students do not get their work done, as these students are self-motivated learners. These students, in the rare instance

that they don't follow procedures, will accept consequences without attitude and are always honest with the teacher. Type 1 students are often the most academically successful students. Should these students ever need a call home (which is usually unnecessary), the parents are supportive, and the problem stops.

2. Type 2 students are the most complex and are often the most common type of student. They are a "follower" and are heavily influenced by the students around them. If a type 2 student is around a group of type 1 students, he or she will behave like the type 1. Often however, if a type 2 student is around a type 3 student (see below), then he or she will behave like the type 3. Academically, type 2 students vary across the spectrum and follow a typical student talent distribution curve. Most type 2 students get their homework and class work completed. However, if a type 2 student is working with a type 3 student, the assignment tends not to get completed. Type 2 students are generally more willing to accept the consequences of their choices, but some deny that they did anything or give attitude. A phone call home generally receives a positive response from a parent. However, the behavior is less likely to be resolved. It may stop for a few days, but it will eventually come back.

3. Type 3 students are students who rarely make good choices in the classroom. They can't be trusted to make good decisions when left alone. They rarely do their homework, and getting them to complete class work is very difficult, often requiring the teacher to stand in close proximity to them. These students rarely take responsibility for their actions and blame others for their choices. When corrected, these students can become belligerent, attitudinal, or act as if they don't care. These students are frequently bullies and will not hesitate to initiate conflict against their peers and sometimes against their teachers. Many are also highly subversive, not out-and-out causing conflict, but often creating conflict by spreading rumors or instigating others to fight. A phone call home does not solve the problem. These parents have gotten phone calls from their child's teachers for years about the same problems. The sad reality is that many parents of these students have as many issues as the student and can become confrontational with the teacher. Some tell the teacher to never call again, others become verbally abusive, or a few need to be escorted from the building. The other response is nothing. Phone calls are not returned and the parent will not come up to the school to conference with the teacher unless required by the office to do so. Many of the problems of these students can be traced directly to their challenging home environment.

Let's look deeper at some of the social realities of type 3 students. Some live a very uncertain life outside of the classroom with many family issues that most of us can't even imagine. For some of them, going home is not a good thing. We teach children who have been abused, who are or have been homeless, and have little or no parental support. Many times, there is no father in the picture and mom is on welfare or working two, maybe three, jobs just to keep a roof over her family. As a result, here are some of the student behaviors we experience:

1. They have a pronounced "I don't care" attitude.
2. They do not respect much of anyone and certainly not their teachers.
3. They are very difficult to manage in a classroom situation.
4. Their parents often are not involved in many aspects of their educational growth.
5. They do not exhibit an understanding of the value of an education.
6. If parents are contacted about a student issue, and they agree to work with the student, it is often unusual for them to take any action.

As a result of these issues, test scores suffer for the entire classroom/school.

As teachers, we try to reach each and every child. We eat with them, talk one-on-one with them, work with them, and let them know that we genuinely care about them. We see these kids for who they are and try to understand the issues they deal with day in and day out. We know which students have parents going through divorce, which students have a parent in jail or on welfare, or which students have been beaten or abused.

Children are in school about 7 hours each day with only 3.7 hours in instruction time with their teacher in their classrooms. Considering an entire calendar year (365 days), the children are under the direct influence of their teachers about 8 percent of their time. (See appendix D for these time estimates.) With so many problem students, it is very hard for us to deal with the difficult and complicated issues that some of our students have.

Students by Type

Once the definitions for each of the events to be measured were finalized, each teacher was asked to estimate what percentage of their class were the type 1, type 2, and type 3s. After the teachers actually measured the three factors for their classes, we revised the percentages. It is interesting to note that the percentages actually moved up the table after we observed their actual performance. By moving up the table we mean there were fewer 3s, fewer 2s, and more 1s. Table B.1 shows our final estimates of the percentage of our fourth-grade classes by type as well as the number of type 3s in each class

Looking at these numbers one begins to develop a better understanding of what a classroom is like for this D-graded school. With a class size of twenty-four to twenty-five students, these numbers show there will be four to seven

Table B.1. Student Types by Class

Student Type	Teacher (%)				
	1	2	3	4	Averages
1	36	25	37	29	32
2	48	46	42	46	46
3	16	29	21	25	23
					100
Class size	25	24	24	24	
No. of type 3 students	4	7	5	6	

type 3 students in every class. We know that the type 2 students are more highly influenced by the type 3 students than are the type 1 students.

Consequently, a large number of type 2 students will, from time to time, fall into type 3 category. This means that at times, the classroom could have a majority of type 3 students. These situations lead to classroom chaos and severely test the teacher's patience and endurance plus result in sizeable reductions in classroom instruction time. *It is terribly unfair for this small group of type 3 students to deprive the balance of the class from an opportunity to learn and excel.*

Picture yourself as a teacher in one of these classrooms. Teaching had appeal as a profession because of how much influence a teacher can make in a child's life. Your teaching career begins with you full of passion and energy, but you quickly find that far too little of your time is spent teaching. You frequently feel that you are in a constant state of classroom upheaval trying to get control so you can teach.

This is a terrible morale-killer; there must be a way out of this school. Which schools will actually support teaching and have good discipline? Are there schools where the teachers have a say in how things are done? Which schools engage parents to make the school better? Will it ever happen at this school? This may be the time to give up teaching and look for a better skill-fit.

Metrics—Gathering Data

In order to illustrate the nature of the classroom management, we gathered some data. We agreed upon three metrics that are easy to track and to gather daily data for two to three weeks.

The measures are:

1. Multiple requests to follow directions
2. Failure to actively listen
3. Bad attitude/conflict

Here is a more detailed definition of each one of the metrics we will be using in all four classes.

1. Multiple requests to follow directions

Following procedures: Students are following the posted procedures that are discussed and made at the beginning of the year.
Following procedures will be noted whenever the teacher has to ask a student or students to follow procedures or meet expectations more than once.

2. Failure to actively listen

Active listening: Eyes are on the speaker or on the assignment. No side conversations. Students are engaged in the conversation or work. They are not fooling around with something in their desks. They are not creating distractions for the other students or allowing themselves to be distracted.
Failure to actively listen will be noted any time the teacher has to redirect a child to get him or her to pay attention to the lesson.

3. Bad attitude/conflict

Conflict/attitude: Conflict can be anything from one student calling out in class to yell at another student or teacher/adult, two or more students engaged in a verbal altercation, a teacher/adult and student engaged in a verbal altercation, two or more students or teacher/adult and student involved in a physical altercation. This conflict will disrupt the normal flow of the school day by either the conflict occurring during class time or the teacher having to take instructional time to deal with the conflict.
Attitude is being spoken to in a way that is inconsistent with district, school, and classroom expectations.
Conflict/attitude will be noted any time the teacher has to take instructional time to deal with conflict or attitude from a student or students.

Data was collected during the period March 11, 2013, to March 28, 2013. (Note that the teachers have been working with these children for at least six months.) A total of forty-four classroom days was recorded (averaging eleven days per teacher). The teacher recorded data by placing a tally mark on the data sheet under one of these three columns each time the event met the conditions in the definitions:

1. Multiple requests to follow directions
2. Failure to actively listen
3. Bad attitude/conduct

Table B.2.   Total Tally Marks for Each Classroom

	Multiple Requests to Follow Directions	Failure to Actively Listen	Bad Attitude/ Conflict
Classroom 1	253	145	84
Classroom 2	348	207	200
Classroom 3*	91	61	67
Classroom 4	574	113	91
Daily Averages for Each Classroom			
Classroom 1	19	11	6
Classroom 2	29	17	17
Classroom 3	10	7	7
Classroom 4	49	7	10
Overall average	**26**	**11**	**10**

*Teacher 3 was absent for two days due to illness during the data-gathering period.

A total of 2,054 tally marks were recorded along with, in two classes, the name/initials of the offending students if the students were classified as a type 2 or 3. Table B.2 shows the summary of the tally mark data.

In order to clarify these data, let's take a look at two of the numbers. The upper array—the 253 tally marks—was recorded in Classroom 1 for multiple requests to follow directions. This means that over the thirteen days that this teacher recorded data; he/she marked down 253 tally marks to record the 253 instances. Teacher 3 recorded 91 tally marks for the nine days he/she recorded data. As you can see, there are different numbers of recording days; so total tally marks are not the best for drawing conclusions.

The second array records daily averages over the full reporting period and considers only the days when data was recorded. The 19 in the second array is the average per day number of events for teacher 1, while teacher 3's average was 10.

The best numbers to use are the overall average since they blend all the teachers together. We see that the typical classroom averaged twenty-nine occasions/day when a student was told multiple times to follow directions. The really important events are the time-consuming actions that must be taken when students need to be managed for their bad attitude or conduct—there were ten of these events each day for each class. All three of the different events take the teacher away from teaching instructional content and replace this time with nonproductive classroom-management matters.

Loss of Instruction Time

In appendix D, we show the time analysis for a typical school, in this case an A-graded school, since no time has been subtracted for "extraordinary issues." All the disruptions measured above have a negative impact on the basic instructional time of 230 minutes. We have estimated the "loss of instructional time" for each of the factors we measured. Table B.3 shows those estimates.

With these estimates, we can now determine the amount of time lost each day due to problems managing these children.

Table B.4 points out that the three measured classroom management issues take away 62 minutes from the 230-minute instructional day—this is a 27 percent drop, a loss that no student can afford. (On an annual basis, this is about 186 hours of lost instruction time.) We believe this time loss and the associated classroom disruptions do not contribute to a "learning environment" and are the major reasons our students did not do well on their assessment exams.

We now ask what portion of this is coming from the type 3 students? Fortunately, two of the four teachers recorded their data in such a way that we can deduce what percentage of the sixty-two minutes calculated above is attributed to the small number of type 3 students. Analysis shows that 59.6 percent of the lost instructional time for each of the two classes is originating with the type 3 students. We will assume that this percentage applies to all four classes. Calculating, we compute that $0.596 \times 62 = 37$ minutes of lost instructional time is coming from the type 3 students.

The vast majority of this lost thirty-seven minutes is coming from attitude/conflict. We will dig deeper into this area. Analysis shows that 73 percent of the total type 3 time comes from attitude/conduct—this is

Table B.3.   The Duration of an Event

Measured Disruption	Time Loss in Minutes/Event
Multiple requests to follow directions	0.5
Failure to actively listen	0.25
Bad attitude/conflict	4.5

Table B.4.   Calculating Total Lost Instructional Time

Measured Disruption	Time Loss in Minutes/Event	Average No. of Events/Day	Lost Instructional Time in Minutes/Day
Multiple requests to follow directions	0.5	26	13
Failure to actively listen	0.25	11	3
Bad attitude/conflict	4.5	10.23	46
Total lost time/day			62

Table B.5.   How the Sixty-Two Minutes Breaks Out by Student Type

	Student Type		
	1	*2*	*3*
Instruction time lost to classroom mgt. in minutes/day	0.9	24.1	37

$0.73 \times 37 = 27$ minutes each day is wasted in dealing with discipline issues from the type 3 students. This is consistent with the definition of the type 3 students.

Table B.5 shows how the classroom management time of sixty-two minutes breaks out for each of the three student types.

Suppose it was possible to suddenly snap our fingers and convert all type 3 students into type 1 students. Not only would we pick up the thirty-seven minutes, we would see a dramatic improvement in the remaining twenty-four minutes since the type 2 students will no longer be influenced by the type 3 students. Since type 1 students need very little classroom management, we would be able to recoup most of the 230 minutes of instructional time we are with the students. This improved time availability, along with a much-improved learning environment, will provide the impetus we need to excel on the standardized exams. We believe that this is one of the primary root causes for the classes' poor test performance.

Is It the Students or the Teachers?

Our data illustrates that we experience a significant loss of classroom instructional time due to the fact that we have so many type 3 and type 2 students that we are unable to control. Aren't some teachers able to manage these problem children? The answer to this question is yes, but they possess some trait, some particular insight or life experience that is so unique that it is not present in most teachers.

After all, looking back over your own educational experience, you can quickly identify a small number of those very gifted teachers who really excited you about learning. But there are not many who possess this special skill; in fact, there are far too few to populate even a small percentage of all the classrooms of America. Most teachers are mere mortals who want to do a good job but don't possess those rare extraordinary talents. Over and over, schools are defining jobs that ordinary teachers are unable to do—this means something is wrong with the job. There are too many children that the teachers just can't control.

What Is the Answer?—The Role of Consequences

In our school, there is a strong reluctance to incorporate consequences into the management of our students. There are no obvious consequences for almost any behavior. It is not uncommon for students to use the "F . . ." word to insult other children, teachers, and administrators. This is one of the ultimate displays of contempt and further establishes the power of the students over those who are the targets of their scorn.

This word, and some like it, may be in common usage in their world outside of school, but it should be totally unacceptable in a system where respect is expected but not demanded. If respect is not a natural result of one's upbringing, it should be demanded at school. Without consequences, nothing will change.

There should be consequences for failure to perform academically. We as teachers work hard to prepare our students for ISTEP and the children ask, "What happens if we fail this exam?" The teachers must be honest and tell them, "Nothing will happen to you but your performance will affect how our school is rated."

A reply like this will have virtually no impact in motivating the student to higher levels of performance. This will be the response in any learning environment at any level. Without personal consequences, motivation is thwarted. There are too many other influences in a student's life to expect learning to become a top priority. We have one recommendation:

> The students would be required to attend a full summer session and then pass an exam to assess if adequate progress has been made. If not, they should repeat the former grade and not be passed on to the next. This is the consequence that may motivate them to make the difficult changes we are looking for.

What Is the Answer?—The Role of Discipline

As teachers, it saddens us to see so many students failing to reach their potential. Their lives could be dramatically improved if we could find ways to increase their learning skills. Looking at the problem simplistically, much improvement could be made if we could convert all type 3 students into type 1 or 2 students. Here are some suggestions:

1. Elevate the level of discipline with the objective of moving many of the type 2 students to type 1 catagory. There must be consequences for bad behavior. They must be taught that respect for themselves and others will

make their lives more pleasant and self-satisfying. Current methods of discipline are not working; change *must* be made.

2. Likewise, work to elevate as many of the type 3 students to type 2 or even 1 category. Here is where consequences really matter. We cannot continue to allow the type 3 students to have so much negative influence over our classes.

3. Ultimately, there will still be some students who cannot be changed. In our opinion, these students will need to be removed from the classrooms. We strongly believe that removing these children from the classroom will have a strong beneficial effect on the remaining kids. It will most certainly improve student and teacher morale.

4. Establish an alternative school/program for unruly and disruptive children—we comment on this below. If they refuse to attend the socialization program or do attend without changing their behavior and continue to be disruptive, they must be removed from the traditional educational system. We must not let them bring down students who want an education.

As has been pointed out before, there is no question in our minds that the large number of type 3 students leads to a larger type 2 group. The "downward influence" of these students must be stopped.

Looking for "Root Cause"

It would be easy to stop right here and simply resort to the colloquialism, "throw the bums out!" but we would be stopping too early in our quest for the root cause. The question is why they are unruly and create such a problem in class? It seems they do not possess certain social skills and the motivation that we all take for granted, and if they do have the appropriate skills, they are hiding them while in classroom.

Don't forget that social skills are learned just like knowledge skills. These skills are taken for granted because we teach them a little at a time over a large number of years. So, we conclude that there is a major shortfall in these skills that needs to be addressed. Is it too early to expect a fourth grader to be able to change behavior? We don't think so.

It would be very beneficial to the student, future classrooms, and society if they could show more successful social skills earlier in their lives. Here is an area of their growth for the "educational experts" to comment and set a plan in place that will be of major benefit to all concerned. One thing is for sure that it will not be easy to get these children to recognize their deficiencies and spend the time to remedy them.

Our suggestion is that they attend a mandatory summer session either after the third grade or after the fourth to allow the school system to begin to mold them into successful citizens. It would have to be a prerequisite for admittance into the next year's class.

WHAT SKILLS ARE NEEDED TO REMAIN IN THE CLASSROOM?

What is needed is an approach that will provide the skills for these students to live in two different worlds. In addition to their current circumstance, they need the basic skills to allow them to succeed in the world of the classroom; these are skills that will hold them in good stead in the later years in education, in business, governmental jobs, and the military.

Here are some of the skills that must be mastered for a successful return to the classroom:

1. The understanding that education is essential for them to lead a better life.
2. The understanding that even though their circumstances may be far from ideal, they can still be successful if they believe in their teachers and their role in teaching them essential skills.
3. They need to understand why respect of others is so essential for their own success.
4. They need to learn how to manage their behaviors that are brought about because of their life situation.
5. They need to understand the importance of self-discipline and self-motivation.
6. They need to understand what is acceptable speech and what is profane, unacceptable speech.
7. They need to understand how to deal with conflict and how to avoid inflicting either mental or physical harm others.
8. They need to learn the virtue of perseverance and its importance—learning can be hard work.

We can see these are not the ordinary pursuits of a conventionally trained teacher. Topic knowledge is not what these students need at this point; they need to learn successful social behavior and to respect those who need to be respected.

Once the students have satisfactorily demonstrated their grasp of these life skills, they can be returned to the normal tract. From time to time there will be lapses, and the students should be required to attend reminder sessions on Saturdays.

The Last Why

We take the next step and ask, "Why don't these students possess the needed noncognative skills to be successful in the classroom?" The obvious answer is parents/parenting but we don't know this for sure. It could be peer group pressure, culture, or they might deliberately choose to act the way they do. No matter how it happens, it is the way it is, and we must deal with it as such.

There is Hope

As teachers, we know that we can do better. This is a collective "we." With the school administration's help to implement the recommendations suggested above, we know that we can reduce the impact of the type 3 students, the root cause of many of our problems. A by-product of this assistance will be a dramatic improvement in teacher morale and the morale of our students. More importantly, they will begin to reach the levels of success we want them to experience. We know that once the students begin to experience academic success; this success will feed on itself to create a level of pride they have never known.

Without significant change, our school will remain a D-graded school indefinitely. We view this as a "learning tragedy" because so much potential is being wasted.

Richard W. Garrett, PhD
Facilitator Study Completed April 10, 2013

Appendix C

How Much Time Is
Left for Teaching?

At a couple of points in the book, reference is made to the percentage of a day's instruction time wasted by classroom management activities. Table C.1 is the teacher's allocation of how time is used in a typical day. The table begins with the 420 minutes the students are in the school building and begins to subtract noninstructional times, recess, lunch, and so on. Subtracting these times gives 220 minutes that the students are under the teacher in a learning mode.

There are sixty minutes for "out of class" instruction that the teachers did not place in "Classroom instructional time" because this is time with other teachers. These teachers immediately send the children back to their "home room" at the first sign of trouble.

Table C.1. School Time Numbers Used in Study

		Minutes/Day	Percent of Day
Total time students are at school (7 hours)		420	100
Less:	Lunch/recess	75	
	Class start-up	45	
	Out-of-class instruction	60	
	Rest room breaks	20	
Leaving classroom instructional time		220	52
How much of a student's life is under the influence of the school?			
	Hours		Percentages
Total student time per year	8,760		100
Total student time at school	1,260	(180 days/year)	14
Total student instructional time	660	(180 days/year)	8

Notes

2 SOME MAJOR ISSUES IN EDUCATION

1. *Public Education Finances 2014*, US Census Bureau, Top Row of Table 1, https://www2.census.gov/govs/school/14f33pub.pdf.

2. Musu-Gillette, Lauren, and Stephen Cornman, Jan. 25, 2016, *Financing Education National, State and Local and Spending for Public Schools in 2013*, National Center for Education Statistics.

3. During the period 1973–2012, the assessment exams measured performance on the same material and skills. This changed after 2013, so the new data cannot be placed on the same plot.

4. Goldstein, Dana, August 2013, "Why the World Is Smarter than Us," *Daily Beast*, http://www.thedailybeast.com/articles/2013/08/09/why-the-world-is-smarter-than-us.html.

5. *National Rankings Show American Schools Lower: It's Not the Teachers*, It Takes a Village to Teach a Child, Building Bridges between Schools and Parents, http://parents-teachers.com/articles/rankings.shtml.

6. https://www.metlife.com/metlife-foundation/about/survey-american-teacher.html?WT.mc_id=vul101.

7. Ward, Steven C., April 10, 2015, "Why Has Teacher Morale Plummeted?" *Newsweek*, http://www.newsweek.com/why-has-teacher-morale-plummeted-321447.

8. Meador, Derrick, March 07, 2016, "Fun and Effective Strategies for Boosting Teacher Morale," *ThoughtCo.*, http://teaching.about.com/od/admin/a/Fifty-Ways-For-Administrators-To-Boost-Teacher-Morale.htm.

9. Richmond, Emily, March 2012, "Why Are Teachers Dissatisfied with Their Jobs?" *The Atlantic,* https://www.theatlantic.com/national/archive/2012/03/why-are-teachers-dissatisfied-with-their-jobs/254117/.

10. Phillips, Owen, March 30, 2015, "Revolving Door of Teachers Costs Schools Billions Every Year," *nprED*, http://www.npr.org/sections/ed/2015/03/30/395322012/the-hidden-costs-of-teacher-turnover.

11. Ibid.

12. Ibid.

13. Sutcher, Leib, Linda Darlington-Hammond, and Desiree Carver-Thomas, September, 2016, *A Coming Crisis in Teaching?, Teacher Supply, Demand and Shortages in the U.S.*, Learning Policy Institute.

14. Shulman, Robyn, no date given, "Teacher Burnout: Unhappy and Exhausted Teachers; How and Why Everyone Is Affected," *Ed News Daily*, http://www.ednewsdaily.com/teacher-burnout-unhappy-and-exhausted-teachers-how-and-why-everyone-is-affected/.

15. Phillips, Owen, "Revolving Door of Teachers Costs Schools Billions Every Year."

16. Raver, C. Cybele, November 2012, "Low-Income Children's Self-Regulation in the Classrooms: Scientific Inquiry for Social Change," *American Psychologist*, excerpted from paper at various points.

17. *Teaching Interrupted; Do Discipline Policies in Today's Public Schools Foster the Common Good?* 2004, ©Public Agenda, 2004. No reproduction/distribution without permission. www.publicagenda.org; the full report is found at: http://www.publicagenda.org/media/teaching-interrupted, our results are taken from the executive summary.

18. Paul, Tough, 2016, *Helping Children Succeed, What Works and Why*, Houghton Mifflin Harcourt, p. 54.

19. Holcomb, Sabrina, Feb. 17, 2016, "How One Middle School Cut Discipline Referrals by 98 Percent in Just One Year," *NEA Today*, http://neatoday.org/2016/02/17/middle-school-discipline-referrals/.

20. No author listed, April 17, 2016, "Class Action Lawsuit Filed against City Ed Department for Failing to Protect Students from Violence in Schools," *The Bronx Chronicle*, http://thebronxchronicle.com/2016/04/07/class-action-lawsuit-filed-against-city-ed-department-for-failing-to-protect-students-from-violence-in-schools/.

21. Terry, Paul M., "Empowering Teachers as Leaders," University of Memphis, http://www.nationalforum.com/Electronic%20Journal%20Volumes/Terry,%20paul%20M.%20Empowering%20Teachers%20As%20Leaders.pdf.

22. Phillips, Owen, "Revolving Door of Teachers Costs Schools Billions Every Year."

23. Stover, Del, "Is School Board Reform Coming to You?" *American School Board Journal*, http://www.asbj.com/TopicsArchive/Leadership/Is-School-Board-Reform-Coming-to-You.html.

3 WHAT CHILDREN NEED TO SUCCEED

1. There are three other cofounders of Elevate Indianapolis; they are: Jay Height, executive director of the Shepherd Community Center, we talk about his organization in chapter 5; Don Palmer, longtime Indianapolis businessman and community leader, currently managing partner of Honey Creek Capital, LLC; and Bob Whitacre, longtime businessman and Indianapolis community leader, founder and CEO of Cornerstone Companies, Inc.

2. From Steve Cosler, personal communication.

3. The ISTEP exam was redesigned to be more compatible with common core. It turned out to be so difficult that the results for school year 2014–2015 were not useful. It was difficult because of the assumption that the schools were preparing all students to attend a university; this failure led to the demise of the ISTEP exam. Alternatives tests are currently under consideration.

4. Wyman, Nickolas, September 2015, "Why We Desperately Need to Bring Back Vocational Training in Schools," *Forbes.com*, http://www.forbes.com/sites/nicholas-wyman/2015/09/01/why-we-desperately-need-to-bring-back-vocational-training-in-schools/#7b8a05af465c.

5. Angela Duckworth gleaned from the YouTube video: https://www.youtube.com/watch?v=H14bBuluwB8. She recently published a book *GRIT, The Power of Passion and Perseverance,* Scribner, 2016

6. Espelage, Dorthy, et al., March 2013, "Understanding and Preventing Violence Directed against Teachers," *American Psychologist*, Vol. 68, no. 2, pp. 75–87.

7. Paul Tough is the author of *How Children Succeed, Grit, Curiosity, and the Hidden Power of Character,* Houghton Mifflin Harcourt, 2012 and in 2016, *Helping Children Succeed, What Works and Why,* Houghton, Mifflin Harcourt, 2016.

8. Angela Duckworth is the author of *GRIT, The Power of Passion and Perseverance*, Scribner, 2016.

9. In chapter 4, this student type will be formally defined.

4 THE TEACHERS TELL THEIR STORY—A RESEARCH STUDY

1. Lest you are confused, the total quality process has nothing to do with long-range planning.

2. Johnson, Cynthia, "Leading Learning for Children from Poverty," *Association for Middle Level Education (AIME),* https://www.amle.org/BrowsebyTopic/WhatsNew/WNDet/TabId/270/ArtMID/888/ArticleID/351/Leading-Learning-for-Children-From-Poverty.aspx.

3. For the full list of A-, B-, or C-graded schools, go to website www.failing-school.org/Telling the Story/Indiana Hit Parade of schools. There are 273 in total.

4. Strauss, Valerie, 2014, "A Dozen Problems with Charter Schools," *Washington Post*, https://www.washingtonpost.com/news/answer-sheet/wp/2014/05/20/a-dozen-problems-with-charter-schools/?utm_term=.59a6b54efcd1.

5. Ibid., same web article.

6. BrainJet, no author given, http://www.brainjet.com/random/1525782/teachers-share-their-spine-chilling-student-horror-stories/.

7. Ibid., same website.

8. Smith, Patrick, "12 Teachers Reveal Their Most Horrific Classroom Experiences," *Buzzfeed*, https://www.buzzfeed.com/patricksmith/teachers-reveal-shocking-classroom-stories?utm_term=.btQlNoD2w#.fa0maOxj3.

9. Behman, Elizabeth, January 10, 2016, "Classroom in Crisis: Violence Plagues Schools," *TRIBLive*, http://triblive.com/news/education/9709262-74/students-teachers-teacher.

10. Story orally relayed to the author by retired kindergarten teacher from Racine, Wisconsin. She was one of many reviewers of the working research paper.

11. No author listed, October 14, 2014, "Teacher Quits over 'Unruly Kids' and 'Violence in Classrooms,'" *theGRO*, http://thegrio.com/2014/10/30/teacher-quits-over-unruly-kids-and-violence-in-classroom/.

12. The ISTEP-oriented instruction time of 220 minutes does not include music, art, or computer training; these topics were covered outside of the usual classroom by other instructors. Any hint of misconduct will cause the instructor to dismiss the students back to their regular classroom.

13. Source: http://www.whitehouse.gov/the-press-office/2013/05/17/remarks-first-lady-bowie-state-university-commencement-ceremony.

14. http://www.publicagenda.org/pages/who-we-are.

15. *Teaching Interrupted*, executive summary.

5 LOOKING FOR A SOLUTION

1. Tough, Paul, *Helping Children Succeed*, p. 58.

2. Ibid., p. 57.

3. Schneider, Chelsea, and Stephanie Wang, December 15, 2016, "Teacher Bonus Pay Favors Rich Districts," *Indianapolis Star*, p. 3A.

4. Wang, Stephanie, and Chelsea Schneider, December 22, 2016, "Teachers Make the Most of 'Insult,'" Indianapolis Star, p. 3A.

5. Tough, Paul, *Helping Children Succeed*, p. 61.

6. St Benedictines Prep School of Newark, NJ. On 6/26, *60 Minutes* featured a great story on this most unusual school. The website for the *60 Minute* show is http://www.cbsnews.com/news/60-minutes-newark-school-st-benedicts-scott-pelley/.

7. Johnson, Cynthia, no date given, "Leading Learning for Children from Poverty: Six Effective Practices Can Help Teachers Help Students from Poverty Succeed," *AIME Assn. for Middle Level Educators*, https://www.amle.org/BrowsebyTopic/WhatsNew/WNDet/TabId/270/ArtMID/888/ArticleID/351/Leading-Learning-for-Children-From-Poverty.aspx.

8. National Institute for Early Education Research, http://nieer.org/research/state-preschool-2015.

9. Richmond, Emily, May 2013, "Guest Post: Economist James Heckman on Long Dividends of Early Learning Investment," *Educational Writers Association*, http://www.ewa.org/educated-reporter/guest-post-economist-james-heckman-long-dividends-early-learning-investment.

10. "Importance of Early Childhood Development," *Encyclopedia of Early Childhood Development*, http://www.child-encyclopedia.com/importance-early-child hood-development.

11. Paul Tough, *Helping Children Succeed*, p. 27.

12. Cook, Tony, and Chelsea Schneider, June 4, 2016, "Pence Reignites Debate over Value of pre-K," *Indianapolis Star*, p. 1.

13. James Heckman, http://www.brainyquote.com/quotes/authors/j/james_heckman.html.

14. Ibid.

15. Ibid.

16. Blumberg, Alex, August 12, 2011, "Preschool: The Best Job-Training Program," *Planet Money,* http://www.npr.org/sections/money/2011/08/12/139583385/preschool-the-best-job-training-program.

17. Barnett, Steven, PhD, March 20, 2013, *The True Value of ECE* (Early Childhood Education), Rutgers Graduate School of Education, National Institute for Early Education Research.

18. Ibid.

19. Clothier, Steffanie, and Julie Poppe, *New Research: Early Education as Economic Investment*, National Conference of State Legislatures, http://www.ncsl.org/research/human-services/new-research-early-education-as-economic-investme.aspx.

20. Whitehurst, Grover J., February 26, 2014, *"Does Pre-K Work? It Depends How Picky You Are,"* The Brown Center Chalkboard Series Archive | Number 56 of 115 Paper | February 26, 2014, http://www.brookings.edu/research/papers/2014/02/26-does-prek-work-whitehurst.

21. Stevens, Katharine B., and English, Elizabeth, 2016, "Does Pre-K Work? The Research on Ten Early Childhood Programs—And What It Tells Us?" The American Enterprise Institute, p. 34.

22. Much of this material comes from the report *Shepherd Community: An Assessment*, by Dr. Amy L. Sherman from the Sagamore Institute for Policy Research, Indianapolis, July 2015.

23. The website for the 60 Minutes show is: http://www.cbsnews.com/news/60-minutes-newark-school-st-benedicts-scott-pelley/. To view you must belong to 60 Minutes All Access. Here is a free YouTube video: https://www.youtube.com/watch?v=HepSmBnDL2g. Another YouTube video: https://www.youtube.com/watch?v=vzxpWVdIG_Y.

24. Paul Tough, 2016, *Helping Children Succeed, What Works and Why*, Houghton Mifflin Harcourt, p. 73.

6 DRAMATIC IMPROVEMENTS ARE NEEDED

1. With great confidence, I will assure you that once a school achieves success with the *disruptive* students, they will adopt much of their curriculum to be used in all classes.

APPENDIX B

1. Indiana Statewide Testing for Educational Progress.

2. Source: http://www.doe.in.gov/achievement/assessment/istep-results.

About the Author

Prior to this book, **Richard W. Garrett's** most significant publication (coauthored with Dr. John R. Virts) was an article in the *Harvard Business Review* titled "Weighing Risk in Capacity Expansion."

Garett began his academic career at DePauw University but decided to leave premed after two years to become an engineer. He is a trained industrial engineer, BS and MS (Purdue), and has a PhD in operations research (Northwestern University). He has twenty-seven years of business experience with Eli Lilly and Company, a large pharmaceutical company. Beginning in 1994, having retired from Lilly, he was an associate clinical professor at the Kelley School of Business, Indiana University, Bloomington, and during the same period, he was a partner in a consulting firm.

During his six and one-half years at IU, he won an award for designing the most innovative new course in the MBA program. During ten years of his working career, he served as an accreditor of engineering departments around the country through ABET.

During his years at Eli Lilly, he was one of the corporate leaders in the use of the Total Quality process—the process used in this study. He has facilitated approximately sixty long-range plans for nonprofit groups in central Indiana. He is the founder of the website www.elevateteachers.org.